WALL PILATES WORKOUTS FOR WOMEN

50 Complete Video Tutorials and Illustrations to Lose Weight, Gain Confidence, and Get the Body You Want - 28-Day Ab Transformation Challenge Included

By Evi Matonis

© Copyright—Evi Matonis 2024—All rights reserved.

The content contained within this book may not be reproduced, duplicated, or transmitted without direct written permission from the author or the publisher.

Under no circumstances will any blame or legal responsibility be held against the publisher or author for any damages, reparation, or monetary loss due to the information contained within this book, either directly or indirectly. You are responsible for your own choices, actions, and results.

Legal Notice:

This book is copyright-protected. This book is only for personal use. You cannot amend, distribute, sell, use, quote, or paraphrase any part of the content within this book without the author's or publisher's consent.

Disclaimer Notice:

Please note the information contained within this document is for educational and entertainment purposes only. All efforts have been made to present accurate, up-to-date, reliable, and complete information. No warranties of any kind are declared or implied. Readers acknowledge that the author is not engaging in rendering medical or professional advice. The content within this book has been derived from various sources.

Published by: Evi Matonis
Contact me: evimatonis@gmail.com

Ebook ISBN: 978-1-915710-68-0

Paperback ISBN: 978-1-915710-69-7

Hardcover ISBN: 978-1-915710-70-3

HOW TO ACCESS THE VIDEO DEMONSTRATIONS

1. Get the password from the chapter titled 'Video Demonstrations Password' at the end of this book.
2. Scan the QR code below with your phone.
3. Enter the password.

If you have any issues accessing the videos, please email me at evimatonis@gmail.com. Good luck, and I wish you all the best with your wall Pilates practice!

TABLE OF CONTENTS

Introduction — 1

Welcome! 1
What is Pilates? 1
Traditional Pilates vs. Wall Pilates 2

Wall Pilates Benefits and Prep Work — 4

The Benefits of Wall Pilates 4
How to Modify Wall Pilates Exercises 5
Pilates Exercise Fundamentals 5
Learning the Fundamentals, Cues, and Their Meanings 8
Lifestyle Changes and Weight Loss Essentials 9
Preparation for Your Workout 13

Wall Pilates Exercises — 15

Warm-Up 15
Upper Body 28
Lower Body 42
Core 74

28-Day Ab Transformation Challenge — 116

Workout #1: Low-Intensity 117
Workout #2: Moderate-Intensity 117
Workout #3: High-Intensity Interval Training (HIIT) 117
Workout #4: Mix and Match 117
Workout #5: Arm Day 117
Workout #6: Leg Day 118
28-Day Workout Calendar 118
Exercise Quick Reference Table 119

Conclusion: Plan for Consistency — 121

Video Demonstrations Password — 122

References — 123

INTRODUCTION

Welcome!

Pilates has gained awareness and increased interest by fitness enthusiasts over the past 30 years. In addition to improving strength, mobility, and body composition, it promotes the mind-body connection many seek on their health and wellness journey. While Pilates may have been primarily used as a form of rehabilitation from injury, modern Pilates is now used the world over by everyone from professional athletes to celebrities and people like you and me.

Pilates was created by Joseph Pilates as a way to strengthen weak, injury-prone bodies and improve body conditioning. The primary concept of Pilates was to develop a coordinated connection between the brain and body, to enhance awareness and muscle coordination, and to deepen the effectiveness of traditional small-movement exercises.

What is Pilates?

Pilates' surprising history intertwines artistic expression, innovation, and rehabilitation. It all began in the early 20th century with German-American Joseph Pilates, who had a diverse background in bodybuilding, gymnastics, and entrepreneurship. Pilates initially crafted the exercise program out of his love for health as a means to recover from injuries.

Unlike other energetic routines that were demanding and taxing on the body, Pilates involved controlled movements that were done on a mat while prone or supine and sometimes in sitting positions. These small movements were aimed at developing abdominal muscles believed by Pilates to be fundamental to overall stability and suppleness.

By 1914, Pilates' life had changed forever; he had become a prisoner of war, serving time in confinement on the Isle of Man. While incarcerated, Pilates observed his surroundings, specifically noting the movements of the cats that inhabited the island, and began formulating a series of stretches, testing these on himself and his fellow confinees.

To his surprise, these stretches not only improved his range of motion but also his overall strength and mental well-being—and Contrology was born. With the cornerstone of Pilates's philosophy now established, he began to develop several apparatuses beyond the mat. These unique tools, like the Reformer and the Cadillac, were designed to deepen stretches and strengthen and align exercises initiated on the mat.

Pilates wrote down his method in two small yet influential books. "Your Health: A Corrective System of Exercising That Revolutionizes the Entire Field of Physical Education" (1934) and "Return to Life Through Contrology" (1945). The works became a base for future trainers and demonstrated Pilates' self-devotion toward teaching others and improving people's lives through physical training.

Many exercise forms or disciplines have evolved from this original Contrology methodology, but Pilates' foundational ideas remain the same. The foundational principles that shape a workout are crucial for fostering a mind-body connection and ensuring optimal results, which include:

- Centering

- Concentration
- Control
- Breath
- Precision
- Fluidity

Whether called Contrology or Pilates, the focus is on exercise performance to move intentionally with purpose. Pilates is a mindful discipline. Each principle is utilized during your exercise session.

Today, Pilates is not just a method of rehabilitating people; instead, it has become one of the most popular forms of exercise, with more than 12 million regular practitioners worldwide. Pilates appeals to people from all walks of life, especially those seeking to improve core strength, become more flexible, and have better balance.

While Pilates may not have been specifically designed for women, it is the ideal gentle, low-impact exercise to help lose weight, rehabilitate from injury and a sedentary life, and reclaim health and well-being.

TRADITIONAL PILATES VS. WALL PILATES

Traditional Pilates follows an order of exercises involving the entire body, performed in multiple positions to attain different muscle activity and joint movements. It may be performed using equipment or simply a mat on the floor. Initially, you use only your body's resistance. Exercises can then progress by adding resistance through weights, bands, or classic equipment such as the Reformer or Cadillac.

Wall Pilates has become popular recently as the fitness industry continues to adapt to challenge health-conscious people and their fitness goals. How is wall Pilates different from traditional Pilates? The difference is that wall Pilates mainly involves using the wall for support or resistance while maintaining the basic principles and concepts of conventional Pilates.

One attraction to wall Pilates is that you can practice it in your home, making it a more accessible option for some than attending studio classes. Wall Pilates raises the bar from a basic mat program, which is challenging in its own right. Using a wall to create resistance adds another dimension to your workouts and challenges your body.

Pilates has a wide range of benefits that will be discussed in the following section, but its beauty lies in its flexibility. Exercises can be adapted to meet a person's needs and limitations, making workouts safe and effective. The best approach for beginners is to start with easier variations that will help increase basic strength and control. For example, pregnant women or those who have recently given birth can modify their workouts by focusing on strengthening their pelvic floor and core.

Pilates offers a safe, complementary practice to traditional physiotherapy for those who have suffered injuries, reducing recovery time and increasing overall strength. At-home Pilates does not require a specific instructor, but we do need to work within our limitations, choosing to listen to our bodies and adapting each movement as needed.

Before we move on to the other powerful benefits of Pilates, allow me to introduce myself. My name is Evi Matonis, and I am a trained mat Pilates instructor who has taught and practiced the discipline for over 15 years. I'm also a licensed physical therapist assistant and have personally and professionally benefited from Pilates principles and exercises. It is my pleasure to share with you what I have learned over the years, given the profound impact I know it can have on people's lives. I know how amazing a regular Pilates routine can make you look and feel. I hope that everyone reading this book experiences those same wonders. Now, let's get onto the benefits of Pilates and how to prepare for your workout.

WALL PILATES BENEFITS AND PREP WORK

THE BENEFITS OF WALL PILATES

While many of you who have purchased this book already know the incredible impact Pilates can have on your well-being, some of you may still be wondering, *"Why should I be practicing Pilates?"*

Aside from the well-known benefits such as improved appearance, enhanced well-being, reduced injury risk, and increased mindfulness, your personal reasons for practicing Pilates could vary widely. Indeed, pinpointing why Pilates is beneficial for you specifically can be challenging, as it deeply depends on your individual goals. Many people struggle to recognize what their body needs or believe they don't have the time to properly care for themselves due to their hectic daily routines.

For many people, desk jobs can lead to poor posture, worse fitness, and weakened muscles without them even noticing. Pilates principles focus on the conditioning of the muscles that support us structurally and improve posture and tolerance for everyday activities. The concepts of traditional Pilates encourage strength, mobility, and thoughtful balance throughout our whole bodies, ensuring we begin undoing the sedentary habits we have formed.

And it's this focus on our postural support that ultimately begins to develop the foundational muscles we have long neglected, improving support of the spine and pelvic areas. Additionally, Pilates exercises move your body in a manner that helps lengthen and stretch muscles. These movement patterns align and balance the body, improving your structural support.

Strengthening your core can reduce the risk of injury by preventing muscle imbalances that lead to strains, sprains, and tears. A stronger core and better posture can protect you. Studies indicate that Pilates is particularly effective in alleviating chronic pain and enhancing functionality for people suffering from conditions such as lower back and neck pain.

Regular Pilates practice offers physical benefits that enhance and reinforce movement patterns used in everyday activities. Functional movement patterns include twisting, bending, reaching, pulling, and pushing. These movements are essential for most people's daily activities and crucial for many athletes as well. This training approach readies your body for movement in every direction.

Regularly practicing Pilates can tone muscles, aid in weight loss, boost muscle mass, and enhance your physical appearance. By using resistance and body weight to stretch and strengthen, Pilates encourages the development of long, lean muscles, fortifying the body's essential support system. This leads to a more aesthetically pleasing physique and increased strength for daily activities.

Wall Pilates often leads to noticeable improvements in posture, strength, balance, and weight management, thanks to the use of a wall. This simple tool acts as support for those needing stability and provides resistance without requiring specialized equipment. Incorporating resistance into exercises intensifies muscle activation and introduces dynamic movements, engaging both small and large muscle groups effectively.

Finally, the advantages of Pilates go beyond the physical. Regular practice has been proven to improve mental health, increasing "feel-good" hormones like endorphins that increase feelings of well-being. The combination of controlled movements, focused breathing, and relaxation techniques used in Pilates helps ease anxiety and effectively manage stress. The mindfulness aspects of the movements help bring awareness and focus.

How to Modify Wall Pilates Exercises

The true potential of Pilates is unlocked by aligning it with our personal goals and acknowledging our limitations. For beginners or those with movement restrictions, wall Pilates offers a welcoming gateway to discovering the strength and versatility of our bodies.

Through the safety of the wall and the added resistance, we can progress as our bodies become stronger, fitter, leaner, and more stable. Pilates doesn't focus on explosive, complex, or difficult-to-follow movements or require hours-long workouts. Instead, each movement is designed to precisely target specific muscle groups. This means that regardless of our flexibility or fitness levels, we can modify the exercises, deepening stretches to where we are comfortable while focusing on technique. The true beauty of wall Pilates is, however, in using the wall as a way to increase and decrease the intensity of each movement. Foot placement, tilt, and the angles at which we place our bodies can significantly alter the challenge of a movement.

So, how do we modify our workouts?

If you're a beginner on your wall Pilates journey, you should focus on mastering foundational movements and techniques while using props like rolled towels or pillows to support the body and ensure proper alignment. This will allow you to concentrate on maintaining correct posture and engaging the targeted muscle groups without straining or overexerting yourself.

Once you have gained confidence and strength, you can gradually reduce your reliance on props and start using the wall to increase each movement's intensity. For example, a beginner might start with a simple wall squat, keeping their back against the wall and feet hip-width apart for support. As they progress, they can move their feet further away from the wall, increasing the angle of their body and engaging more muscles in the legs and core. Advanced wall Pilates practitioners can take their practice to the next level by incorporating additional movements that target multiple muscle groups simultaneously. The beauty of wall Pilates lies in its adaptability, allowing everyone to gradually progress at their own pace.

Pilates Exercise Fundamentals

There are several important concepts to be aware of in Pilates.

What Is the Core?

The core comprises crucial muscles that stabilize and support the spine, pelvis, and torso. These muscles work together to maintain proper posture, balance, and body alignment during movement. They primarily consist of the abdominal muscles, back muscles, and hip muscles.

The abdominal muscles, including the rectus abdominis (the "six-pack" muscles), transverse abdominis (the deepest abdominal muscle), and obliques (side abdominal muscles), help flex and rotate the torso. They also provide support and stability to the spine and pelvis during various movements.

The back muscles, like the erector spinae and multifidus, help extend and rotate the spine. These muscles work in conjunction with the abdominal muscles to maintain proper posture and prevent excessive arching or rounding of the back.

Finally, the hip muscles, including the glutes and hip flexors, are also considered part of the core. They help stabilize the pelvis and provide power for movements like walking, running, and jumping.

A strong and stable core is essential for several reasons, including injury prevention, improved posture, enhanced performance when moving, and better balance and stability. Using wall Pilates ensures we target all these fundamental core muscles to improve our stability and strength.

Pilates Principles Explained

We briefly touched on the six principles previously. These principles are the fundamental ideas enacted throughout a Pilates exercise session, which help you focus and bring awareness to your body during the practice.

Centering

Centering is based on learning how to engage your foundation muscles—the main focus in Pilates. What are the foundation muscles? A simple way to explain this is the foundation = the core.

In Pilates, these muscles are called "the powerhouse" and are essential for your body's structural support. Muscles surrounding your spine, shoulder blades (or scapula), and pelvis give the body a solid platform that allows positive movement patterns. Remember: A strong foundation can withstand almost any storm.

When learning to engage your core correctly, you must become aware of the techniques you use. Engaging your core means tightening your transverse abdominal muscles. You will be cued to bring your navel inward toward your spine, "navel to spine," "scoop the belly," or "hollow out your belly" are all common phrases in Pilates.

The goal is to draw your abdominal muscles toward your spine for support rather than pushing your stomach out. Activating your abs in this manner creates a supportive brace for your spine during exercise. Engaging the transverse abdominis, the deepest abdominal muscle, also activates the multifidus muscles in the back, which are essential for spinal stability.

When the transverse abdominis and multifidus muscles contract together, they offer muscular support that stabilizes the spine. Mastering this technique is crucial for correctly performing Pilates exercises and maximizing the benefits of the practice.

Concentration

The mind-body connection while performing Pilates originates through concentration. Focusing on each movement, combined with breathing, deepens your practice. This principle is important to attain the mind's control over the body and is necessary to be present in your workout.

Control

Now that you are centered and concentrating on your exercises, you must learn to control every movement. This task is challenging since it requires continuous re-focusing when the mind wanders. Pilates' control principle is an exercise in mindfulness, willing your muscles and bones to move intentionally. The principle of control involves consciously directing your whole body with clarity and deliberateness so you become immersed in every exercise.

Breath

Breathing in Pilates involves being mindful of how your body moves. When you inhale, your diaphragm and ribs expand. When you exhale, they contract, leading to the tightening of your abdominal muscles. Imagine a balloon: as you inflate it, it expands, and as you let the air out, it deflates.

A practical method to learn breathing awareness is lying comfortably on your back with your hands resting on your upper chest and belly. Take a breath inward, and as you inhale, notice your belly and chest rise and then fall as you exhale. Inhale, and the balloon expands; exhale, and the balloon deflates.

In Pilates, you'll be instructed to inhale deeply to fill your lungs and then exhale forcefully to expel all the air. With each forceful exhale, your belly contracts, pulling your navel toward your spine. This breathing technique is used with every exercise repetition, emphasizing the importance of the principles mentioned earlier and focusing your attention on them.

Specific exercises require a slightly different breathing pattern; two to five inhalations are followed by the same number of exhalations for each repetition or set of exercises. The overall breathing concept is the same, but the pace will be faster. Pilates breath work is crucial for achieving optimal benefits.

Precision

Moving your body in precise motions is the essence of Pilates. Every arm reach or leg lift has a purpose and thus should be executed as precisely as possible. Your mind concentrates solely on that movement at that time before moving on to the next. That sounds like a perfectionist agenda, right? Not exactly. More so, it is a lesson in patience and striving toward a laser-focused effort one rep at a time.

Fluidity

In traditional Pilates, an ordered series of exercises are performed to flow from one to the next, with each body part working in succession. Mat-based and equipment-using classes normally follow this format. However, instructors may alter the exercise order to suit their students' needs. Fluidity in wall Pilates may also differ since many exercises are modified for wall use.

Whatever form of Pilates you choose, the principle remains meaningful in that you intend to strive for a flow of movement throughout your practice. No singular muscle action or exercise is done without a purpose.

The takeaway is that each principle is revisited in a cyclical pattern throughout your practice, proving why Pilates is the ultimate mind-body discipline, constantly refocusing you on your body and its movements. It is also why Pilates may be the most beneficial form of activity for body conditioning and rehabilitation.

Learning the Fundamentals, Cues, and Their Meanings

In wall Pilates, understanding and applying fundamental cues is essential for engaging the core muscles effectively and maintaining proper form throughout your practice.

1. **Navel to spine:** This cue reminds you to engage your deepest abdominal muscle, the transverse abdominis. By gently drawing the navel toward the spine, you create a supportive corset around your midsection, stabilizing the lumbar spine and pelvis. In wall Pilates, this engagement helps maintain a neutral spine position against the wall.
2. **Breathing with rib expansion**: Proper breathing techniques are crucial in Pilates, and wall Pilates is no exception. Focus on lateral breathing, which involves expanding the ribcage to the sides during inhalation and gently contracting the ribs during exhalation. This breathing pattern helps engage the deep core muscles and promotes relaxation of the neck and shoulders.
3. **Imprinting the spine:** This cue involves gently pressing the lower back against the wall or floor, creating a slight posterior pelvic tilt. By imprinting the spine, you engage the abdominal muscles and minimize the arch in the lower back, promoting a neutral spine position. This is particularly important in wall Pilates exercises that require a stable and supported spine.
4. **Long spine:** Maintaining a long spine refers to creating space between each vertebra and avoiding excessive arching or rounding of the back. In wall Pilates, this cue helps practitioners maintain a tall, neutral posture while engaging the core muscles to support the spine. Imagine lengthening through the crown of your head and tailbone simultaneously.
5. **Shoulder blades toward the ribcage:** This cue encourages practitioners to slide their shoulder blades down the back, away from the ears, and gently press them into the wall. By doing so, you engage the muscles between the shoulder blades (middle trapezius and rhomboids) and promote a stable and open upper body posture. This is especially important in wall Pilates exercises that involve arm movements.
6. **Lower ribs toward the pelvis:** This cue is a reminder to avoid flaring the lower ribs, which can occur when the core muscles are not adequately engaged. You maintain a neutral spine position and engage the abdominal muscles more effectively by gently drawing the lower ribs toward the pelvis. This cue is instrumental in wall Pilates exercises challenging core stability, such as leg lifts or single-leg balance poses.

Incorporating these fundamental cues into your wall Pilates practice helps you better understand core engagement and proper form. As you progress, these cues will become second nature, allowing you to focus on the flow and intensity of your movements while maintaining a strong, stable core.

The Importance of Warm-Ups

Warming up is crucial to any exercise routine, including wall Pilates. Taking 5 to 10 minutes to properly warm up your body before engaging in exercise can provide numerous benefits and help you get the most out of your practice.

The primary goal of a warm-up is to gradually increase your heart rate and blood flow, which raises your body temperature. As your body warms up, your muscles become more pliable and receptive to stretching and contracting, reducing the risk of injury and allowing for a greater range of motion during your workout. A proper warm-up should consist of simple, low-intensity movements that engage the major muscle groups you'll use during your wall Pilates session. These movements can include marching in place, shoulder rolls, hip circles, and light dynamic stretches. However, I have provided you with a comprehensive warm-up program that allows your cardiovascular system to adapt and prepare for the upcoming exercises.

In addition to preparation and injury prevention, proper warm-ups can help enhance your mental focus, improve coordination, and provide a boost of energy to help keep you motivated throughout your workout.

Remember, the key is to warm up your body, not exhaust yourself before you've even begun your wall Pilates routine. Your aim is to allow your body to adapt and prepare for the upcoming session and lay the foundation for a safer, more effective, and enjoyable wall Pilates practice.

LIFESTYLE CHANGES AND WEIGHT LOSS ESSENTIALS

We've discussed the benefits and fundamentals of Pilates for your body and mind. Improving your body composition or muscle-to-fat ratio is an especially inviting perk of adding wall Pilates to your life. If your intention is weight loss, then lifestyle changes are necessary.

Diet and Nutrition

Nutrition plays a vital role in maintaining a healthy lifestyle, yet it is often overlooked or forgotten at the expense of exercise. While regular physical activity is crucial for overall health and well-being, it is equally important to understand that a balanced and nutritious diet is essential for optimizing the benefits of your fitness routine.

Proper nutrition gives your body the energy, vitamins, minerals, and other essential nutrients to fuel your workouts, support muscle recovery, and maintain overall health. Without adequate nutrition, your body will struggle to perform at its best during exercise, and you will experience fatigue, muscle weakness, or even injury.

Having said that, it's essential to recognize that there is no one-size-fits-all approach to nutrition. Each person has unique needs based on age, gender, body composition, activity level, and health status. What works for one person may not necessarily work for another, and it's crucial to listen to your body and adapt your diet accordingly.

There are, however, some core principles that everyone should follow.
- **Eat a variety of nutrient-dense foods:** Focus on incorporating a wide range of fruits, vegetables, whole grains, lean proteins, and healthy fats into your diet. This diversity ensures that you're getting a broad spectrum of essential nutrients.
- **Stay hydrated:** Drinking enough water is crucial for maintaining proper bodily functions, regulating body temperature, and supporting exercise performance. Aim to drink at least 8 glasses of water daily, and more if you're engaging in intense physical activity.
- **Be mindful of portion sizes:** While the quality of your food choices is important, so is the quantity. Pay attention to portion sizes and listen to your body to avoid overeating.
- **Limit processed and high-sugar foods:** Processed foods and those high in added sugars often lack essential nutrients and can contribute to weight gain and other health issues. While it's okay to enjoy these foods in moderation, focus on whole, minimally processed foods as the foundation of your diet.

- **Don't forget about pre and post-workout nutrition:** What you eat before and after your wall Pilates sessions can impact your performance and recovery. Aim for a balanced meal or snack containing carbohydrates and protein before your workout, and replenish with a protein-rich meal or snack within an hour post-exercise to support muscle recovery and repair.

A Word on Liquid Calories

Liquid calories are consumed through soda, fruit juices, sports drinks, sweetened teas, and alcohol. While these drinks can be enjoyable and provide some hydration, they often contain added sugars and empty calories that can quickly add up and contribute to weight gain and other health issues.

Many of these drinks can cause issues with our nutrition because:
- **They contain high sugar content:** Many beverages, especially sodas and fruit juices, are high in added sugars. Consuming excessive amounts of sugar can lead to weight gain, diabetes, and other chronic health problems.
- **They are filled with empty calories:** Liquid calories often lack essential nutrients like vitamins, minerals, and fiber. They may satisfy thirst or provide a quick energy boost, but they don't contribute to overall nutrition or feelings of fullness.
- **They unknowingly increase our calorie intake:** It's easy to consume many calories through beverages without realizing it. For example, a 12-ounce can of soda contains about 150 calories, and a 16-ounce sweetened coffee drink can have up to 400 calories or more.
- **They reduce feelings of fullness**: Liquid calories don't trigger the same feelings of fullness as solid foods. As a result, you may consume more calories overall without feeling satisfied.

Remember, finding an approach that works for you and your needs is the key to a sustainable and healthy diet. Don't be afraid to experiment with different foods and eating patterns until you find a balance that makes you feel energized, satisfied, and able to support your wall Pilates practice and overall health goals. Consult a registered dietitian or healthcare professional for personalized guidance if you have specific nutritional concerns.

Physical Activity

Exercise in some form is necessary to achieve a healthy lifestyle. It's important to note that to lose weight, you should combine adequate nutrition alongside 150 minutes of moderate-intensity exercise each week.

Moderate intensity is, however, different for every person.

The formula for individual target heart rate and intensity level is as follows:
- 220 - Age = Maximum Heart Rate (MHR) in beats per minute (bpm).
- For Target Heart Rate range (THR) at moderate intensity: MHR x 64% and 76%.
- Example: 220 - 40 = 180 bpm MHR.
- 180 x 64% = 115 bpm.
- 180 x 76% = 137 bpm.

If you do not have a heart rate monitor or smartwatch, you can find your heart rate by counting bpm at pulse points on the side of the neck between the ear and collar bone or the inside of the wrist on the thumb side.

Daily physical activity is ideal for managing a healthy lifestyle. That likely means varying types of activities on different days. Walking, bike riding, weight training, running, swimming, and Pilates are all great options for activities.

It could also entail parking further from your destination, climbing the stairs instead of taking the elevator, and cleaning your house from top to bottom. Reducing your daily sitting time so that your overall life is less sedentary is better for your long-term health.

Nutrition, Exercise, and Weight Loss

When it comes to weight loss, it's important to understand that it requires a multifaceted approach that involves both a healthy diet and creating a calorie deficit. In simple terms, to lose weight, you need to consume fewer calories than your body burns.

A calorie deficit occurs when you consume fewer calories than your body needs to maintain its current weight. This can be achieved by reducing calorie intake or increasing physical activity levels. Wall Pilates, for example, can be an effective way to increase your calorie expenditure while also building strength and improving overall fitness. You will need to consider a couple of key points regarding a calorie deficit for weight loss.

1. **Determine your current calorie needs:** To create a calorie deficit, you must first know how many calories your body needs to maintain its current weight. This can be estimated using online calculators or by consulting with a healthcare professional or registered dietitian.
2. **Set a realistic calorie deficit:** Aim to create a modest calorie deficit of 250 calories per day. This can typically be achieved by reducing your calorie intake by 125 calories and burning an additional 125 calories through exercise. A gradual, moderate approach is more sustainable and healthier than extreme calorie restriction.
3. **Focus on nutrient-dense foods:** When reducing your calorie intake, it's crucial to focus on nutrient-dense foods that provide essential vitamins, minerals, and fiber. Opt for whole grains, lean proteins, fruits, vegetables, and healthy fats while minimizing processed and high-calorie foods.
4. **Incorporate physical activity:** Regular exercise, such as wall Pilates, can help you burn additional calories and support your weight loss efforts. Aim for at least 150 minutes of moderate-intensity exercise per week.
5. **Be consistent and patient:** Weight loss is a gradual process that requires consistency and patience. Stick to your healthy eating and exercise plan, and don't get discouraged if you don't see immediate results. Celebrate smaller victories, such as improved energy levels, better sleep, and increased strength and flexibility.

Remember, while creating a calorie deficit is essential for weight loss, it's equally important to approach it in a balanced, sustainable way. Crash diets or extreme calorie restriction can lead to nutrient deficiencies, muscle loss, and a slowed metabolism, making it harder to lose weight in the long run. Combining a healthy, nutrient-dense diet with regular physical activity like wall Pilates and creating a modest calorie deficit can support your weight loss goals and improve your overall health and well-being. Consult a healthcare professional before starting a new diet or exercise program if you have any underlying health conditions or concerns.

Sleep Importance

While a balanced diet and regular exercise, like wall Pilates, form the foundation of a successful weight loss journey, another crucial factor often goes overlooked: sleep. Sleep quality is essential for maintaining a healthy weight and supporting overall well-being.

Research has shown that insufficient sleep can disrupt the delicate balance of hormones that regulate appetite and hunger. When you're sleep-deprived, your body produces more ghrelin, a hormone that stimulates appetite, and less leptin, a hormone that signals fullness. This hormonal imbalance can lead to increased cravings for high-calorie, processed foods and make it harder to feel satisfied after eating, ultimately contributing to weight gain.

In addition to its impact on appetite hormones, lack of sleep can also affect your metabolism, the process by which your body converts food into energy. Studies suggest that sleep deprivation can decrease insulin sensitivity, making it more difficult for your body to regulate blood sugar levels effectively. This metabolic disruption can hinder your body's ability to burn calories efficiently, further impeding weight loss efforts.

The consequences of inadequate sleep extend beyond just weight management. When you're tired, finding the energy and motivation to engage in physical activity can be challenging, which is crucial for weight loss. Moreover, sleep deprivation can impair cognitive function, making it harder to make healthy food choices and stick to your weight loss plan. Elevated stress levels, another common side effect of sleep deprivation, can also contribute to unhealthy eating habits.

Aim to get 7 to 9 hours of quality sleep each night. Establish a consistent sleep schedule, create a relaxing bedtime routine, and ensure that your sleep environment is comfortable and conducive to rest. By combining a balanced diet, regular wall Pilates practice, and sufficient, high-quality sleep, you'll be well on your way to achieving your weight loss goals and maintaining a healthy lifestyle.

Stress Management

While diet and exercise are the most well-known aspects of weight loss, another factor can significantly impact your progress—stress. Chronic stress has become a common obstacle for many people trying to achieve and maintain a healthy weight.

When stressed, your body produces cortisol, an important hormone in managing stress. However, high cortisol levels can lead to weight gain through two main mechanisms. Firstly, cortisol can cause intense cravings for sugary and high-carbohydrate foods that offer temporary comfort but can interfere with healthy eating patterns and weight loss goals.

Secondly, high cortisol levels can interfere with your sleep quality. As we now know, poor sleep can negatively impact your metabolism and lead to unhealthy food choices, further complicating your weight loss journey.

By acknowledging the role of stress in weight loss and taking proactive steps to manage it, you can create a more balanced approach to achieving your health goals. Remember, the journey to a healthier lifestyle is not just about the numbers on the scale; it's about nurturing your physical, mental, and emotional well-being. By combining a nutritious diet, regular wall Pilates practice, and effective stress management techniques, you'll be well-equipped to overcome obstacles and achieve lasting success in your weight loss journey.

Final Thoughts

Various lifestyle and wellness factors, such as mental and physical health conditions, can impact your weight loss and fitness objectives. These challenges might seem overwhelming, yet the flexibility of wall Pilates allows for benefits beyond rapid weight loss. Adopting a softer and more mindful exercise method enables you to gain strength, flexibility, and balance without excessive strain on your body or mind.

It's essential to consider the role of medication in your exercise routine. Some medicines can affect your body's performance, causing side effects like dizziness or fatigue that may impact your ability to practice wall Pilates safely. By having an open conversation with your healthcare provider about your medications and any potential side effects, you can work together to create a plan that supports your overall health and wellness.

Remember, your well-being should always be the top priority in your wall Pilates practice. If you feel unwell or experiencing unusual symptoms, consult a healthcare professional before continuing your exercise regimen. By listening to your body, communicating with your healthcare team, and making necessary adjustments to your practice, you can create a strong, sustainable foundation for your wall Pilates journey.

Embracing wall Pilates as part of a holistic approach to health means honoring your unique needs and challenges, both physical and mental. With patience, self-compassion, and a commitment to your well-being, you can unlock the transformative power of this practice, experiencing the joy and vitality that comes from nurturing your body, mind, and spirit in equal measure.

PREPARATION FOR YOUR WORKOUT

You've read the basics about Pilates and the importance of looking at your lifestyle and making healthy changes. Now it's time to organize your wall Pilates workout. Let's dive into the how, what, when, and where to prepare.

- First, you'll need an area large enough for your body to move freely but near a wall.
- You will need a non-skid exercise mat, like a yoga mat.
- You should be able to place your mat on the floor perpendicular to the wall.
- You should wear comfortable clothing that allows good mobility.
- Pilates is usually performed in bare feet for better contact and stability.
- Gather small equipment and place it near you so that you can maintain good flow with minimal interruption. Small equipment options include a ball, a ring, dumbbells, and resistance bands.

As you begin, come to your mat with an open mind, leaving behind any preconceived notions about exercise or yourself. This is your time. You should feel encouraged that you are taking steps toward improving your health.

Always remember to do at least a 5 to 10-minute warm-up before beginning any Pilates session. Warm muscles respond better to strengthening and stretching activities, therefore minimizing injuries.

Read through the exercises for optimal comprehension before you start your workout. Don't be afraid to go back and review the introductory chapters whenever you need a refresher. Give yourself time to become familiar with the terminology and concepts.

Work through the exercises eight to 10 times before adding resistance or using small equipment.

You may be surprised that your body and the wall initially provide an effective workout without additional props. It is okay to do a shorter workout than planned; learn to listen to your body.

Once you've read through the chapters, your space is set up, and you're warm, you're ready to go! Welcome to the Pilates world. Have fun!

WALL PILATES EXERCISES

Warm-Up

Once you have completed your 5-10 minute warm-up and blood is pumping, you can begin Pilates warm-up exercises. This series of exercises is to prepare you for specific Pilates movements. They help you become aware of your body's movement and breathing patterns, and you begin to concentrate and center.

Remember: These exercises should not be painful. Never move your body intentionally into a painful position. Pain does not equal a good workout—it means an adjustment may be required or that you are not ready for that exercise.

Breathing and Spinal Alignment

Correct breathing techniques, such as lateral breathing or ribcage expansion, are key to activating deep core muscles, aiding relaxation, and enhancing the mind-body connection. Focusing on your breath helps maintain proper posture, control movements, and optimize exercise benefits. This approach integrates concentration, core engagement, and breathing, teaching you to align your spine correctly.

Steps
1. Start by lying on your back on the floor, placing your hands on your chest and abdomen.
2. Inhale, allowing your abdomen and chest to rise, and feel your ribs expand.
3. Exhale, sensing your hands return to their initial position over your abdomen and chest.
4. Practice this breathing technique for 3-5 minutes to become familiar with the sensation.
5. Pay attention to the feeling of your spine on the floor with each inhalation and exhalation.
6. Visualize your spine gently pressing into the floor, a process known as spinal imprinting, and focus on the sensation of each vertebra.

7. Continue this focused breathing with your spine imprinting into the floor for 2-3 minutes.
8. Stand up and move to a wall. Press your back against it with arms at your sides, feet 6 inches from the wall, and knees slightly bent.
9. While standing, replicate the breathing process, pressing your spine and ribs against the wall for feedback.
10. Attempt to elongate your spine, reaching your head upward toward the ceiling.
11. With your spine against the wall, slide your shoulder blades down toward your ribs.
12. Spend 2-3 minutes in this stance, breathing deeply and concentrating on your spinal alignment.

Modifications

- This exercise can be adapted for sitting in a chair, on the floor, or on a slightly raised surface like a folded towel or pillow.

Problem Solving and Correction

- Problem: Tension and discomfort due to inadvertently engaging neck and shoulder muscles during lateral breathing.

    - *Correction*: Place your hands on the sides of your ribcage to guide your breath and provide tactile feedback. Focus on directing your breath into your hands and expanding your ribs outward rather than upward. With practice, this technique will become more natural and comfortable.

- Problem: Discomfort or strain due to arching or rounding the lower back and not maintaining a neutral spine against the wall.

    - *Correction*: Place a small, folded towel behind your lower back to provide extra support and feedback. Engage your core muscles by gently drawing your navel toward your spine, and focus on maintaining a long, neutral spine throughout your movements. If you still find it difficult, bend your knees slightly to reduce the pressure on your lower back.

- Problem: Compromised alignment and possible discomfort due to holding tension in neck and shoulders.

    - *Correction*: Before each exercise, take a moment to consciously relax your neck and shoulders, allowing them to release away from your ears. If you notice tension creeping in during a movement, pause, take a deep breath, and refocus on keeping your neck long and your shoulders relaxed.

Side Bend Stretch

The Side Bend Stretch, a key exercise in wall Pilates, focuses on the side muscles of your core, enhancing flexibility, strength, and body awareness. It's an effective remedy for the stiffness and tension that comes from long periods of sitting or standing, targeting tightness in the body's sides. By improving the mobility of your torso, this stretch readies you for activities involving twisting, bending, and various functional movements.

Steps

1. Stand with your side facing the wall, extending one arm straight out to press firmly against it.
2. Sweep the other arm outwards and overhead toward the wall in a smooth motion.
3. Begin by inhaling. As you extend your arm overhead, exhale. Inhale once more, feeling the side of your body stretch and lengthen. Return to the starting position with an exhale.
4. Perform the side bend stretch 3-5 times with focused breathing before switching sides.
5. Ensure both feet remain flat and stable on the floor throughout the exercise.
6. Proceed slowly and follow the breathing guidance for optimal results.
7. You should experience a stretching sensation extending from your hip and pelvic area through the side of your ribs, engaging your oblique muscles and lats.

Modifications

- This exercise can be done while seated on the floor or in a chair.

Problem Solving and Correction

- Problem: Hips shifting forward or backward during the stretch compromising your alignment and reducing the effectiveness of the exercise.
  - *Correction*: Before beginning the stretch, ensure your hips are stacked vertically and your body is parallel to the wall. Engage your core muscles to maintain this alignment throughout the movement. If you notice your hips shifting, pause, realign, and continue with the stretch.
- Problem: Tension in your neck and upper back due to hiking up the shoulder on the stretching side toward your ear.
  - *Correction*: Before leaning into the stretch, take a moment to consciously relax your shoulders, allowing them to release away from your ears. As you stretch, focus on keeping your neck long and your shoulders relaxed. If you notice your shoulder creeping up, pause, take a deep breath, and actively release it back down.
- Problem: Undue stress on the spine due to overarching or rounding of the back during the Side Bend Stretch.
  - *Correction*: Before beginning the stretch, find a neutral spine position by gently engaging your core muscles and tucking your tailbone slightly under. Maintain this alignment as you lean into the stretch, focusing on initiating the movement from your waist rather than your lower back. If you find it challenging to maintain a neutral spine, try slightly bending your knees to reduce the pressure on your lower back.

Forward Bend Stretch

This stretch focuses on the muscles along the back of your body, such as the hamstrings, glutes, and lower back. It's an excellent exercise for relieving tension, enhancing flexibility, and promoting balance and harmony within your body. Loosening the muscles in your backside prepares you for movements involving bending or flexing the torso and lower body.

Steps
1. Position yourself an arm's length from the wall, facing it, with one foot ahead of the other, spaced around 1-2 feet apart.
2. Place your hands on the wall and bend your elbows until your forearms are flat against it.
3. Lean forward, pushing your hips back.
4. You'll feel the stretch in the back of your legs, glutes, and back muscles.
5. Take slow breaths, maintaining the stretch for 2-3 full breaths in and out.
6. Do the stretch 3-5 times, alternating the front leg each time.

Modifications
- This stretch can also be done with both feet and legs parallel rather than in a staggered or split stance.
- Instead of bending the elbows, keep the arms straight with the hands pressed against the wall.

Problem Solving and Correction
- Problem: Undue stress on your spine due to rounding of the upper back during the Forward Bend Stretch.
    - **Correction**: Before hinging forward, focus on lengthening your spine, imagining a

string gently pulling the crown of your head toward the ceiling. As you fold into the stretch, maintain this length in your upper back, keeping your shoulders relaxed and your neck long. If you find it challenging to keep your upper back straight, try bending your knees slightly to reduce the tension in your hamstrings and lower back.

- Problem: Unnecessary strain on your joints due to locking your knees, limiting the effectiveness of the stretch.
  - *Correction*: Before folding forward, take a moment to soften your knees, allowing a slight bend to remain throughout the movement. This gentle bend will help protect your joints and allow for a deeper, more comfortable stretch in your hamstrings and lower back.
- Problem: Tension in your neck, shoulders, and upper back due to straining to reach the floor or wall during the Forward Bend Stretch.
  - *Correction*: Remember that the goal of the Forward Bend Stretch is not to touch the floor or the wall but rather to cultivate a sense of release and lengthening in your posterior chain. Focus on hinging forward from your hips, maintaining a neutral spine position, and allowing your arms to hang heavy. If you find yourself straining, ease back into the stretch slightly, prioritizing proper form and alignment over depth.

Chest Opener

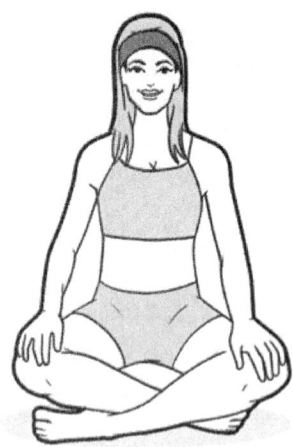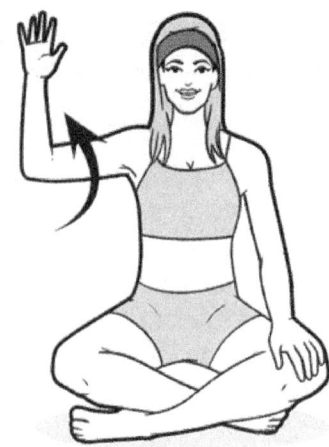

This exercise aims to expand the chest and open the shoulders, encouraging deep and rejuvenating breaths. It's particularly beneficial for correcting poor posture issues like rounded shoulders and a slumped chest, often caused by extended periods of sitting or computer use. Opening the chest improves mobility in the front of the shoulders, addressing tightness from habitual poor posture.

Steps
1. Start by sitting with your back against the wall.
2. Lift one arm to shoulder height, bending it at a right angle like a "goal post," and then reach back to touch the wall.
3. Keep your spine long and sit up straight, ensuring your seat is firmly grounded.
4. Bring your arm back to its starting position in front of you.
5. Breathe in as you open your chest and breathe out as you return to the initial position.
6. Do this movement 3-5 times for each arm.
7. Afterward, try doing the movement with both arms simultaneously for 3-5 repetitions to deepen the stretch.
8. Continuously adjust your posture as necessary to stay upright and tall.

Modifications
- It may be performed in a standing position.
- If you have limited flexibility in your lower body or need better support for maintaining good posture, consider sitting on a folded blanket or pillow for elevation.

Problem Solving and Correction

- Problem: Undue stress on your lumbar spine due to arching of the lower back, compromising the integrity of the movement.
  - ***Correction***: Before beginning the exercise, take a moment to find a neutral spine position by gently engaging your core muscles and tucking your tailbone slightly under. Maintain this alignment as you raise your arms and press into the wall, focusing on keeping your lower back in contact with the wall throughout the movement. If you find it challenging to maintain a neutral spine, try slightly bending your knees to reduce the pressure on your lower back.
- Problem: Tension in your neck and upper trapezius muscles due to shrugging your shoulders toward your ears during the Chest Opener.
  - ***Correction***: Before raising your arms, take a moment to consciously relax your shoulders, releasing them away from your ears. As you press into the wall, focus on keeping your shoulders relaxed and your neck long. If you notice your shoulders creeping up, pause, take a deep breath, and actively release them back down.

Double Arm Reach

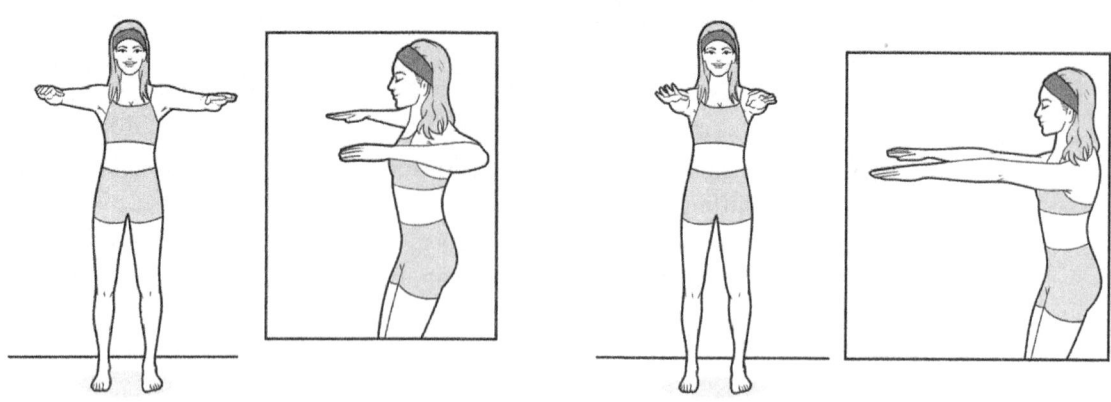

This dynamic wall Pilates exercise simultaneously engages the upper body and core. It's designed to better your posture, boost shoulder mobility, and improve your body's overall alignment and coordination. The movement activates your upper back, shoulders, and chest muscles, facilitating a warm-up. It also teaches spinal imprinting during motion and strengthens postural alignment.

Steps
1. Position yourself standing with your back against the wall, feet 6-12 inches from it, and knees slightly bent.
2. Lift your arms straight ahead at shoulder height, ensuring your back remains pressed against the wall.
3. Draw your arms back toward the wall, aiming to touch it with your elbows, then extend them back to the initial position in front of you.
4. Breathe in as you move your arms back and breathe out as you return them to the starting point.
5. Repeat this sequence for a total of 5 repetitions.
6. Keep your spine pressed against the wall throughout the exercise, synchronize your breathing with each movement, and maintain an upright posture.

Modifications
- This exercise can also be done while sitting on the floor, on a raised surface such as a folded towel or pillow, or in a chair.
- For a more challenging variation that tests your mobility, pull your arms back to touch the wall, rotate them into a "goal post" position, and slide your arms up the wall, ensuring they remain in contact with the wall throughout.

Problem Solving and Correction

- Problem: Undue stress on the lumbar spine compromising the integrity of the movement due to arching of the lower back.
  - *Correction*: Before beginning the exercise, find a neutral spine position by gently engaging your core muscles and tucking your tailbone slightly under. Maintain this alignment as you raise your arms overhead, focusing on keeping your lower back in contact with the wall throughout the movement. If you find it challenging to maintain a neutral spine, try slightly bending your knees to reduce the pressure on your lower back.
- Problem: Tension in your neck and upper trapezius muscles due to shrugging your shoulders toward your ears during the Double Arm Reach.
  - *Correction*: Before raising your arms, take a moment to consciously relax your shoulders, releasing them away from your ears. As you reach overhead, focus on keeping your shoulders relaxed and your neck long. If you notice your shoulders creeping up, pause, take a deep breath, and actively release them back down.

Roll-Down

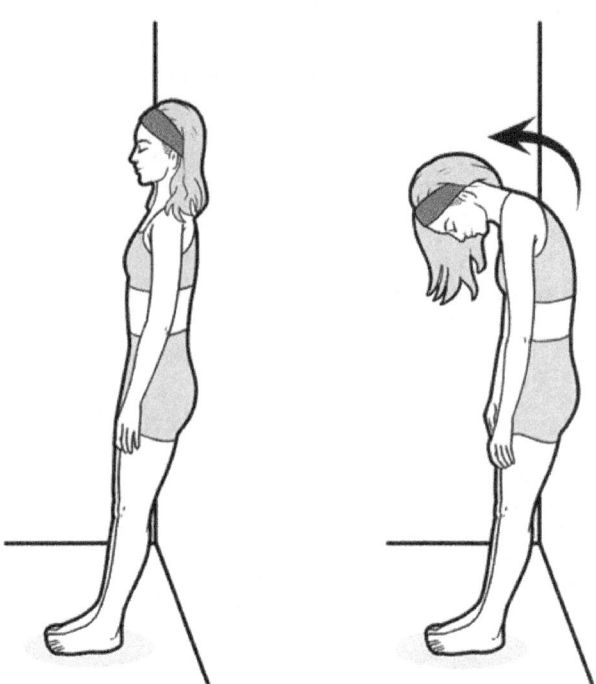

This essential wall Pilates exercise targets spinal flexibility, core stability, and proper posture. It aims to alleviate back tension, improve flexibility, and increase body awareness. The movement specifically develops spinal movement and control while stretching the back and leg muscles.

Steps
1. Position yourself standing with your back to the wall, feet positioned 6-12 inches away, and with a slight bend in your knees.
2. Start with a deep breath in. As you exhale, lower your head, bring your chin toward your chest, and gently round your spine as you bend forward, moving from the top of your spine down toward the floor.
3. Keep your glutes in contact with the wall as you bend.
4. Allow your arms to dangle freely toward the floor as you inhale.
5. On your next exhale, carefully unroll your spine back to standing, inhaling once you're fully upright.
6. Go through this movement 3 times in total.
7. Concentrate on the sensation of each vertebra moving off the wall as you bend forward and rolling back against it as you stand up.
8. Ensure your core is engaged and your navel is pulled toward your spine throughout

the exercise to maintain balance and control.

Modifications
- This exercise can also be done while seated in a chair for added support.
- Adjust the extent of the roll according to your flexibility level.

Problem Solving and Correction
- Problem: Lower back flattening against the wall, compromising the natural curve of your lumbar spine due to excessively tucking your pelvis.
  - *Correction*: Before beginning the exercise, find a neutral pelvis position by gently engaging your core muscles and imagining a subtle lift in your pubic bone. Maintain this alignment as you roll down, focusing on initiating the movement from your upper back rather than your pelvis. If you find it challenging to maintain a neutral pelvis, try slightly tilting your pelvis forward (anteriorly) to counteract the excessive tucking.
- Problem: Losing control and failing to properly articulate through each segment of your spine due to rushing the Roll-Down.
  - *Correction*: Take your time during the Roll-Down, focusing on moving slowly and deliberately. As you roll down, imagine each vertebra peeling away from the wall one at a time, creating a smooth, controlled curve in your spine. Use your breath to guide your movement, exhaling as you roll down and inhaling as you roll up. If you find yourself rushing, pause, reset your focus, and continue with a slower, more mindful pace.
- Problem: Holding tension in your neck and shoulders during the Roll-Down can limit your range of motion and create discomfort in your upper body.
  - *Correction*: Before starting the movement, take a moment to consciously relax your neck and shoulders, allowing them to release any unnecessary tension. As you roll down, keep your chin gently tucked toward your chest to maintain length in the back of your neck. If you notice tension creeping in, pause, take a deep breath, and actively release the tension before continuing the exercise.

UPPER BODY

Standing Plank

This exercise strengthens the core, shoulders, and back muscles, encouraging correct posture and balance. Aimed at enhancing strength, stability, and endurance in the upper body and core, the Standing Plank lays a solid foundation for progressing to more complex Pilates moves. It engages many muscles, including the arms, shoulders, legs, and the entire core (abdominals, hips, glutes, and back). Planks are particularly effective for boosting abdominal strength and stamina, which is crucial for daily activities.

Steps
1. Begin by facing the wall, pressing your hands against it, and spreading your fingers for additional support. Ensure your arms are straight, but keep a slight bend in the elbows to avoid locking them.
2. Step back 1-2 steps until you feel a moderate amount of weight supported by your hands, maintaining straight elbows, and then rise onto the balls of your feet.
3. Take a deep breath in, then draw your navel toward your spine to activate your core muscles as you exhale.

4. Tighten your hip and glute muscles to straighten and slightly angle your body forward, forming a plank position.
5. Keep your neck relaxed and shoulders down, away from your ears, by pulling your shoulder blades toward your ribcage.
6. Maintain this plank position for 3 deep breaths, focusing on keeping your core engaged.
7. To exit the pose, lower from the balls of your feet, walk toward the wall, stand up straight, and gently lower your arms.
8. Aim to complete 5-8 repetitions of this movement.

Modifications

- If wrist discomfort is an issue, try doing planks on your forearms instead of your hands.
- For a more intense workout, move your feet further back from the wall to deepen the angle and balance on the balls of your feet.
- Extending the duration of the plank hold also adds to the challenge.
- For an advanced variation, position yourself with your feet against the wall and your hands on the floor, as in a push-up stance, then press your feet back into the wall to intensify the exercise.

Problem Solving and Correction

- Problem: Undue stress on your lower back due to your hips sagging below the level of your shoulders during the Standing Plank.
  - *Correction*: Before starting the movement, engage your core muscles by gently drawing your navel toward your spine. As you hold the plank position, focus on maintaining a straight line from your head to your heels, actively lifting your hips to align them with your shoulders and feet. If you find it challenging to maintain this alignment, try slightly bending your knees to reduce the difficulty, or take a break and resume the position when you're ready.
- Problem: Tension in your neck and upper back due to hunching your shoulders toward your ears.
  - *Correction*: Before leaning into the plank position, take a moment to consciously relax your shoulders, allowing them to release away from your ears. As you hold the plank, keep your shoulders stacked directly over your wrists, maintaining a sense of space between your ears and shoulders. If you notice your shoulders creeping up, pause, take a deep breath, and actively release them back down.
- Problem: Unnecessary strain on your spine and compromising the neutral alignment of your body due to arching or rounding your back.
  - *Correction*: Before leaning into the plank position, find a neutral spine position by gently engaging your core muscles and imagining a straight line extending from your head to your tailbone. Maintain this neutral alignment while holding the plank, avoiding excessive arching or rounding in your back. If you find it challenging to maintain a neutral spine, try slightly tucking your tailbone under to counteract arching, or take a break and resume the position when ready.

Plank With Arm Reaches

This exercise engages the core, shoulders, back, and arms, enhancing balance, coordination, and control over the entire body. It strengthens the muscles in the arms, shoulders, legs, and core. Additionally, it boosts shoulder mobility and tests your ability to stabilize the spine, thereby improving your functional skills for everyday tasks.

Steps

1. Start with the standing plank position against the wall, following the instructions from the #7 Plank exercise.
2. Begin with an inhale. As you exhale, engage your core by drawing your navel toward your spine and extending one arm upward, away from your body.
3. Inhale as you return the extended arm to the plank position.
4. Exhale and extend the opposite arm away from your body, then inhale as you bring it back to plank.
5. Keep your hips square and facing forward to prevent your body from rotating.
6. Aim for 5-8 repetitions for each arm.

Modifications
- Glide your hands along the wall or limit the reach distance for an easier variation.
- To make the exercise more challenging, step further back from the wall to lower your body angle.

Problem Solving and Correction
- Problem: Compromising the stability and alignment of your body due to allowing your hips to rotate as your arms reach upward.
  - *Correction*: Before starting the movement, engage your core muscles by gently drawing your navel toward your spine. Keep your hips square to the wall as you reach your arm upward, maintaining a stable and aligned position. If you find your hips rotating, pause, reset your alignment, and continue the exercise, focusing on keeping your hips stable.
- Problem: Unnecessary strain on your lower back due to hips sagging below the level of your shoulders and feet as you reach your arm upward.
  - *Correction*: Before reaching your arm forward, ensure that your body is straight from your head to your heels, with your hips aligned with your shoulders and feet. As you reach, maintain this alignment by actively engaging your core and glutes, preventing your hips from sagging or hiking. If you find it challenging to maintain this alignment, try slightly bending your knees to reduce the difficulty, or take a break and resume the exercise when you're ready.
- Problem: Tension in your neck and upper back caused by shrugging your shoulders toward your ears as you reach your arm upward.
  - *Correction*: Before reaching your arm forward, take a moment to consciously relax your shoulders, releasing them away from your ears. Focus on keeping your shoulders stacked directly under your wrists as you reach, maintaining space between your ears and shoulders. If you notice your shoulders creeping up, pause, take a deep breath, and actively release them back down.

Plank Walks

This exercise focuses on strengthening the core, shoulders, back, and legs, enhancing balance, stability, and control of the entire body. It specifically challenges the stability of the spine and the scapula (shoulder blades), reinforcing strength across the core, arms, shoulders, and chest.

Steps
1. Start in a standing plank position with your hands on the wall, your arms extended straight and raised onto the balls of your feet.
2. Take a deep breath, then as you exhale, tighten your core muscles and bend one

elbow to lower that forearm to the wall.
3. Follow by lowering your other arm so that you're in a forearm plank position against the wall.
4. One forearm at a time, press against the wall to straighten your arms back into the starting plank position, inhaling once fully extended.
5. This creates a "walking" motion with your arms, moving from hands to forearms and back, described as down, down, up, up.
6. Keep your body straight and prevent any twisting of the torso. Ensure your core is engaged and focus on your breathing.
7. Complete 5-8 cycles of this movement, alternating the starting arm each time.

Modifications

- To increase the difficulty, walk your hands lower down the wall to create a sharper angle with your body, placing more weight on your arms.
- For an added challenge, complete two rounds of the exercise, starting with one arm leading and then switching to the other arm leading for the second set.

Problem Solving and Correction

- Problem: Compromised stability and alignment of your body due to allowing your hips to shift from side to side as you step your arms during Plank Walks.
  - *Correction*: Before starting the movement, engage your core muscles by gently drawing your navel toward your spine. Keep your hips stable and aligned with your shoulders and feet as you step backward. Imagine your body is a solid plank, moving smoothly and steadily without excessive swaying or shifting. If you find your hips shifting, pause, reset your alignment, and continue the exercise, focusing on keeping your hips stable.
- Problem: Unnecessary strain on your lower back due to sagging your hips below the level of your shoulders.
  - *Correction*: Before starting the Plank Walks, ensure that your body is straight from your head to your heels, with your hips aligned with your shoulders and feet. As you step your feet backward, maintain this alignment by actively engaging your core and glutes, preventing your hips from sagging or hiking. If you find it challenging to maintain this alignment, try slightly bending your knees to reduce the difficulty, or take a break and resume the exercise when you're ready.

Plank Shoulder Taps

This movement strengthens the core, shoulders, back, and arms, enhancing balance, control over your movements, and concentration. It specifically builds strength in the arms, shoulders, and core while promoting stability in the shoulder blades and spine.

Steps
1. Start in a plank position with your hands against the wall, keeping your arms straight and rising onto the balls of your feet.
2. Breathe in, and as you exhale, draw your navel toward your spine to activate your core.
3. Lift one hand from the wall and tap the opposite shoulder with it.
4. Place that hand back on the wall and repeat with the other hand, tapping the opposite shoulder.
5. Continue alternating taps on the fronts of your shoulders with each hand.
6. Maintain core strength throughout and avoid twisting your body.
7. Perform this alternating shoulder tap sequence for 5-8 cycles.

Modifications
- To make the exercise more challenging, position your plank lower on the wall, increasing difficulty by adjusting your body's angle.
- Increase the number of sets to two or three for an additional challenge.
- For a less intense option, lift your hand off the wall without reaching across to the opposite shoulder.

Problem Solving and Correction

- Problem: Compromising the stability and alignment of your body due to allowing your hips to rotate as you tap your shoulders, placing undue stress on your lower back and hips.
  - *Correction*: Before starting the movement, engage your core muscles by gently drawing your navel toward your spine. As you tap your shoulders, keep your hips square to the wall and maintain a stable and aligned position. If you find your hips rotating, pause, reset your alignment, and continue the exercise, focusing on keeping your hips stable.
- Problem: Compromising the integrity of the exercise and placing strain on your lower back due to sagging your hips below the level of your shoulders.
  - *Correction*: Before starting the Plank Shoulder Taps, ensure that your body is straight from your head to your heels, with your hips aligned with your shoulders and feet. As you tap your shoulders, maintain this alignment by actively engaging your core and glutes, preventing your hips from sagging or hiking. If you find it challenging to maintain this alignment, try slightly bending your knees to reduce the difficulty, or take a break and resume the exercise when you're ready.

Push-Up

This classic exercise is a proven method for building strength in the chest, shoulders, triceps, and core. Push-ups specifically target and fortify the arms, chest, and core while also enhancing the stability of the shoulder blades and spine.

Steps
1. Start in a plank position with your hands pressed against the wall, your arms extended and raised onto the balls of your feet.
2. Take a deep breath in and out, activating your core muscles.
3. As you breathe in, gently bend your elbows to bring your body closer to the wall, maintaining control over the movement.
4. Lower yourself only to a point where you can maintain good form.
5. Push back against the wall, extending your arms to return to the starting position while exhaling.
6. Ensure your body remains straight and your core stays engaged throughout the exercise.
7. Complete 5-10 repetitions of this movement.

Modifications
- Adjust your plank position to be lower on the wall, making the exercise more challenging.

- Introduce a second set of repetitions for an added challenge.
- To make the exercise easier, stand closer to the wall and minimize the bending of your elbows.

Problem Solving and Correction

- Problem: Undue stress on your spine due to arching of your lower back.
  - *Correction*: Before you start the movement, ensure that your core is engaged and you have rotated your pelvis so your tailbone is tucked in. Hold focus as you lower toward the wall, keeping your core engaged while maintaining the proper breathing pattern. Maintaining proper breathing with a tight core can be challenging at first, but it becomes easier with practice.

Single Arm Push-Up

This powerful exercise boosts strength, stability, and control on one side by focusing on the chest, shoulder, core, and triceps. Performing push-ups with a single arm isolates the movement, allowing for targeted muscle engagement and helping to address and correct any muscular imbalances.

Steps
1. Start in a plank position against the wall, keeping your arms close to your body instead of fully extended.
2. Take a deep breath, then exhale and engage your core by drawing your navel toward your spine.
3. Move one arm off the wall to rest it on your hip.
4. With an inhale, gently bend the elbow of the arm still on the wall, performing a partial push-up.
5. Push back from the wall while exhaling to return to the starting position.
6. For added balance, extend the opposite leg back like a kickstand.
7. Maintain control throughout the movement, ensuring your hips and shoulders stay aligned with the wall, your core remains engaged, and your breathing is steady.
8. Do 5-8 repetitions before switching to the other arm.

Modifications
- Given the difficulty of this exercise, consider attempting it once you've completed 5-10 Pilates sessions.

- For a greater challenge, position yourself further from the wall.
- Introduce a second set of repetitions to increase the difficulty.

Problem Solving and Correction

- Problem: Undue stress on your lower back and shoulders by allowing your hips or shoulders to rotate as you perform the movement.
    - *Correction*: Before starting the movement, engage your core by gently drawing your navel toward your spine. As you lower yourself toward the wall, keep your hips and shoulders square and maintain a stable and aligned position. If you find your hips or shoulders rotating, pause, reset your alignment, and continue the exercise, focusing on maintaining a neutral body position.
- Problem: Undue stress on the shoulder and decreased effectiveness of the exercise due to flaring your elbow out to the side as you lower yourself.
    - *Correction*: As you lower yourself toward the wall, keep your elbow close to your body, pointing it toward your feet at a 45-degree angle. This will help target your chest, shoulder, and triceps more effectively while reducing the risk of shoulder strain. If you find your elbow flaring out, pause, reset your alignment, and then continue the exercise with a focus on keeping your elbow close to your body.

Tricep Side Push-Up

This variation of the classic push-up targets the triceps alongside the stabilizing muscles of the upper body and core. It aims to strengthen the triceps in the upper arm, as well as the core and shoulder muscles.

Steps
1. Start by kneeling on your side, with one shoulder close to the wall and the arm furthest from the wall extended across your body to press your hand against the wall.
2. The arm nearer to the wall should be wrapped around your waist.
3. Lean toward the wall by bending the elbow of the arm that's pressing against the wall, performing a sideways push-up with one arm.
4. Follow the breathing pattern of inhaling as you lower yourself toward the wall and exhaling as you push back to the starting position.
5. Ensure your body stays straight, engage your core muscles, and control the movement to prevent any twisting of the torso.
6. Repeat the exercise 5-8 times for each arm.

Modifications
- This exercise is advanced and can be skipped until you can execute it with proper form and control.
- The difficulty level is influenced by how far your body is from the wall; adjust your position to suit your ability.
- Introduce a second set for an additional challenge.

Problem Solving and Correction

- Problem: Unnecessary strain on your lower back caused by sagging your hips below the level of your shoulders.

    - ***Correction***: Before starting the Tricep Side Push-Up, ensure that your body is straight from your head to your knees, with your hips aligned with your shoulders and feet. As you lower yourself toward the wall, maintain this alignment by actively engaging your core and glutes, preventing your hips from sagging or hiking.

- Problem: Undue stress on your shoulder and decreased effectiveness due to flaring your elbow out to the side or forward as you lower yourself.

    - ***Correction***: As you lower yourself toward the wall, focus on keeping your elbow close to your body and pointing down. This will help isolate your triceps more effectively while reducing the risk of shoulder strain. If you find your elbow flaring out or pointing forward, pause, reset your alignment, and then continue the exercise with a focus on keeping your elbow close to your body and pointing behind you.

Lower Body

Pro tip: Do this group of exercises with bare feet for better stability and to avoid slipping.

Standing Leg Kicks

This exercise focuses on the glutes, hamstrings, and core, enhancing balance, coordination, and strength in the lower body. It also uses the arms, shoulders, and scapula for stabilizing support. Additionally, it improves hip flexibility, which is beneficial for individuals who spend a lot of time sitting.

Steps
1. Start by standing with your face toward the wall and place your hands on it. Walk your feet back until your body forms an L shape with the wall.
2. Press firmly into the wall with your hands, straighten your arms, and push your hips back to extend your spine and secure your stance.
3. Breathe in, and as you exhale, tighten your core by drawing your navel toward your spine.
4. On your next inhalation, lift one leg straight back, keeping it level with or below the height of your hips.
5. Exhale and gently lower the leg back to the floor.
6. Maintain even shoulders and hips, avoiding any rotation of the upper body or arching of the back.
7. Perform the leg lift 10 times before switching to the other leg.

Modifications
- For additional support, do this exercise in a more upright stance.

- To make it more challenging, perform another set of repetitions or use a resistance band around your ankles.

Problem Solving and Correction

- Problem: Undue stress on your lumbar spine and compromised core stability due to arching your lower back as you kick your leg behind you.

    - ***Correction***: Before starting the movement, engage your core muscles by gently drawing your navel toward your spine. As you kick your leg back, focus on maintaining a neutral spine position and keeping your hips level. If you find yourself arching your lower back, pause, reset your alignment, and continue the exercise, focusing on maintaining a stable core and neutral spine.

- Problem: Decreased exercise effectiveness due to leaning forward or backward as you kick your leg behind you, causing you to lose your balance.

    - ***Correction***: Before starting the Standing Leg Kicks, ensure that your body is upright, with your shoulders stacked over your hips and your weight evenly distributed between your feet. As you kick your leg back, maintain this upright posture by engaging your core and keeping your shoulders relaxed. If you find yourself leaning forward or backward, pause, reset your alignment, and continue the exercise, focusing on maintaining an upright, stable posture.

Standing Side Leg Kick

This exercise focuses on the side muscles of the hips, thighs, and core, such as the gluteus medius, abductors, and obliques, to strengthen the hips, legs, and core. It increases hip flexibility, making it particularly beneficial for those who lead a more sedentary lifestyle.

Steps
1. Start by standing and facing the wall. Lower your hands down the wall until your body forms an L shape. Keep your arms straight, press firmly into the wall, and extend your hips back.
2. Breathe in, and as you breathe out, tighten your abdominal muscles.
3. Inhale once more while lifting your leg to the side, keeping it straight at the knee.
4. Exhale and gently bring your leg back down to the floor.
5. Ensure your hips and shoulders remain even, without any twisting of the body.
6. Avoid any swinging motions with your leg.
7. Perform the side leg raise 10 times before switching to the opposite leg.

Modifications
- You can do this exercise in a more upright posture for additional stability.
- To make it more challenging, either complete a second set of repetitions or use a resistance band around your ankles.

Problem Solving and Correction
- Problem: Losing balance as you kick your leg out to the side reduces the effectiveness of the exercise.

- *Correction*: Before starting the movement, engage your core muscles by gently drawing your navel toward your spine. As you kick your leg out to the side, focus on maintaining a tall, upright posture and keeping your hips level. If you find yourself leaning to the side, pause, reset your alignment, and continue the exercise, focusing on maintaining a stable, vertically aligned upper body.
- Problem: Undue stress on your lumbar spine and compromised stability of your core due to arching or rounding of your lower back as you kick your leg to the side.
  - *Correction*: Before starting the Standing Side Leg Kick, ensure that your spine is in a neutral position, with your pelvis neither tucked nor tilted. As you kick your leg out, maintain this neutral spine position by engaging your core muscles and avoiding excessive arching or rounding in your lower back. If you find it challenging to maintain a neutral spine, try slightly reducing the height of your kick or focusing on a more controlled, precise movement pattern.

Standing Side Leg Circles

This active wall Pilates movement concentrates on the hips, thighs, and core, specifically engaging the gluteus medius, abductors, and obliques. It aims to fortify the muscles in the hips, legs, and core while also improving hip flexibility and stabilizing the spine.

Steps
1. Start by standing and facing the wall, then walk your hands down until you're halfway between standing upright and being in an L position against the wall.
2. Use your hands to press against the wall for stability.
3. Take a deep breath in, and as you exhale, engage your core by drawing your navel toward your spine. Inhale again and lift your leg, beginning to trace a semi-circle outward.
4. Complete the circle with your leg as you exhale.
5. Ensure your hips and shoulders remain level, keep your core engaged, and avoid any twisting of the upper body or undue arching of the back. Move your leg and hip with control.
6. Do 5-10 circles with your leg moving backward, then switch to making forward circles. After completing both directions, switch legs and repeat the sequence.

Modifications
- Stand more upright and make smaller circles with your leg for an easier version.
- Add more repetitions, perform a second set, or assume a deeper L position against the wall to increase the challenge.

Problem Solving and Correction

- Problem: If your circles are inconsistent in size or shape, it can indicate a lack of control or stability in your hip and thigh muscles.
  - *Correction*: Focus on tracing circles consistent in size and shape, prioritizing precision and control over speed or range of motion. Visualize drawing perfect circles with your leg, engaging your hip and thigh muscles to maintain a stable, controlled movement pattern. If you find it challenging to maintain consistency, try tracing smaller circles or reducing the number of repetitions until you build greater strength and control.
- Problem: Difficulty maintaining balance while performing the Standing Side Leg Circles can make the exercise frustrating or uncomfortable.
  - *Correction*: If you struggle with balance, try placing your hand closer to your body on the wall for added support. Focus on engaging your core muscles and maintaining a stable support base through your standing leg. You can also try tracing smaller circles or reducing the number of repetitions until you build greater strength and stability. As you progress, gradually increase the size of your circles and the number of repetitions as your balance and stability improve.

Wall Squat

This basic wall Pilates move concentrates on strengthening the legs, hips, and core, especially the quadriceps, glutes, and lower back. It enhances muscular endurance and helps improve performance in everyday activities like climbing stairs.

Steps
1. Start by placing your back against the wall, then step your feet 1-2 feet away from the wall.
2. Take a deep breath in, and as you breathe out, draw your navel toward your spine to engage your core.
3. Slide down the wall into a squat, aiming for your thighs to be parallel to the floor and your knees to be bent at a 90-degree angle.
4. Maintain this position for 2-3 breaths, keeping your core tight, then smoothly slide back up to your starting stance.
5. Ensure your spine remains straight and pressed against the wall throughout the exercise.
6. Perform the squat 5-10 times.

Modifications
- Introduce arm raises either forward or to the sides while squatting to make the exercise harder (like in the illustration).
- Remaining higher up on the wall will make the squat easier.
- Extend the duration you hold the squat position to add more intensity.

Problem Solving and Correction

- Problem: Undue stress on your knee joints caused by extending your knees beyond your toes as you lower into the squat.
  - *Correction*: As you lower into the squat, focus on sitting back into your hips as if lowering yourself onto a chair. Keep your weight evenly distributed through your feet, with your heels firmly planted on the ground. If your knees extend beyond your toes, adjust your foot position or limit your squat depth until you can maintain proper alignment.
- Problem: Undue stress on your lumbar spine caused by the rounding or arching of the lower back as you perform the Wall Squat.
  - *Correction*: Before starting the Wall Squat, ensure that your spine is in a neutral position, with your head, shoulders, and hips in contact with the wall. As you lower into the squat, maintain this neutral spine position by engaging your core muscles and avoiding any excessive rounding or arching in your lower back. If you find it challenging to maintain a neutral spine, try limiting the depth of your squat or focusing on a more controlled, precise movement pattern.
- Problem: Shifting your weight onto your toes as you perform the Wall Squat can compromise your balance and reduce the effectiveness of the exercise in targeting your leg and hip muscles.
  - *Correction*: As you lower into the squat, focus on keeping your back in contact with the wall and your weight evenly distributed through your feet, with your heels firmly planted on the ground. Avoid letting your upper body lean forward, or your weight shift onto your toes. If you find yourself leaning or shifting, pause, reset your alignment, and continue the exercise, focusing on maintaining a stable, upright posture.
- Problem: If you experience knee pain or discomfort while performing the Wall Squat, it may indicate an underlying issue or improper form.
  - *Correction*: If you experience knee pain, check your alignment and ensure that your knees align with your toes and do not extend beyond them. If pain persists, try limiting the depth of your squat or placing a small exercise ball between your lower back and the wall for added support. If pain continues or worsens, stop the exercise and consult a qualified Pilates instructor or healthcare professional for personalized guidance.

Partial Squat With Leg Extension

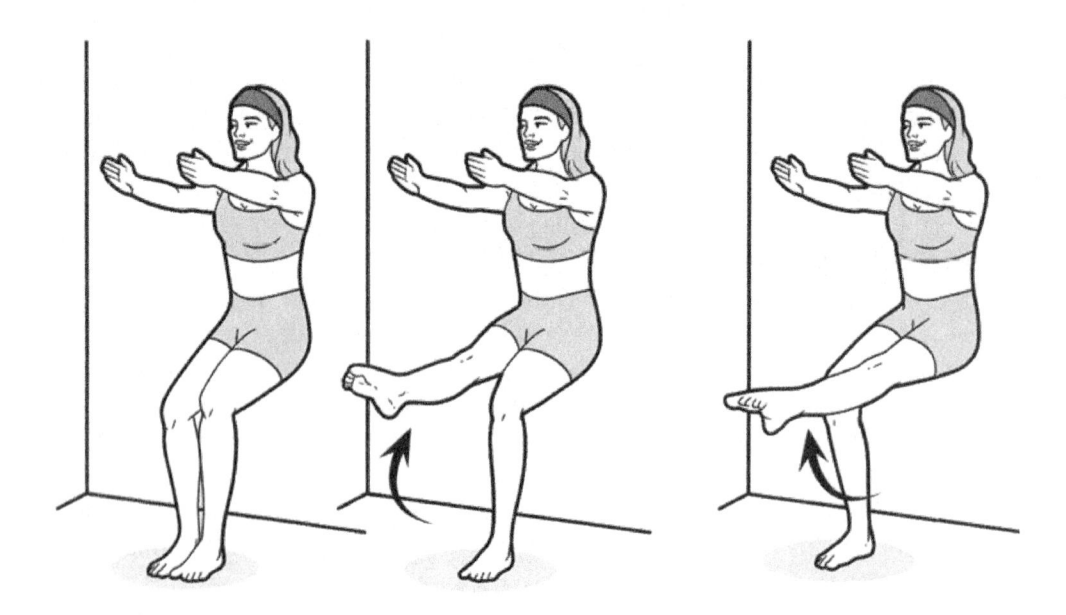

This wall Pilates movement blends a gentle squat with an extension of one leg, engaging the leg, hip, and core muscles. It aims to strengthen these areas, boosting core, leg, and hip muscle power. Additionally, it enhances muscular endurance, helping you perform daily activities more efficiently.

Steps
1. Start by standing with your back against the wall and step your feet forward 1-2 feet away from it.
2. Breathe in, then as you breathe out, tighten your core muscles and lower yourself into a half squat by sliding down the wall.
3. With another inhale, prepare, then extend one leg forward away from the wall as you exhale. Bring the leg back to the half-squat stance as you inhale. Exhale while switching to extend the other leg.
4. Keep your spine pressed against the wall, engage your core, and ensure your hips stay even throughout the leg extensions.
5. Alternate extending each leg for 3-5 repetitions, then slide up to return to your initial standing position. Complete 2-3 sets of this sequence.

Modifications
- For an easier version, reduce the squat depth or decrease the distance you extend your leg.
- Adjust the number of sets up or down to match the level of challenge you desire.

Problem Solving and Correction

- Problem: Compromised balance and effectiveness of the exercise for targeting your leg and hip muscles due to leaning forward or shifting your weight forward when performing the exercise.
  - *Correction*: As you lower into the squat and extend your leg, focus on keeping your back in contact with the wall and your weight evenly distributed through your supporting foot, with your heel firmly planted on the ground. Avoid letting your upper body lean forward, or your weight shift onto your toes. If you find yourself leaning or shifting, pause, reset your alignment, and continue the exercise, focusing on maintaining a stable, upright posture.
- Problem: Rotating or shifting your hips as you extend your leg forward can compromise the core's stability and the exercise's effectiveness in targeting your leg muscles.
  - *Correction*: Keep your hips level and squared to the wall as you extend your leg forward. Engage your core muscles and avoid any rotation or shifting in your hips. If you find your hips rotating or shifting, pause, reset your alignment, and continue the exercise, focusing on maintaining a stable, neutral hip position.

Partial Squat With Knee Lift

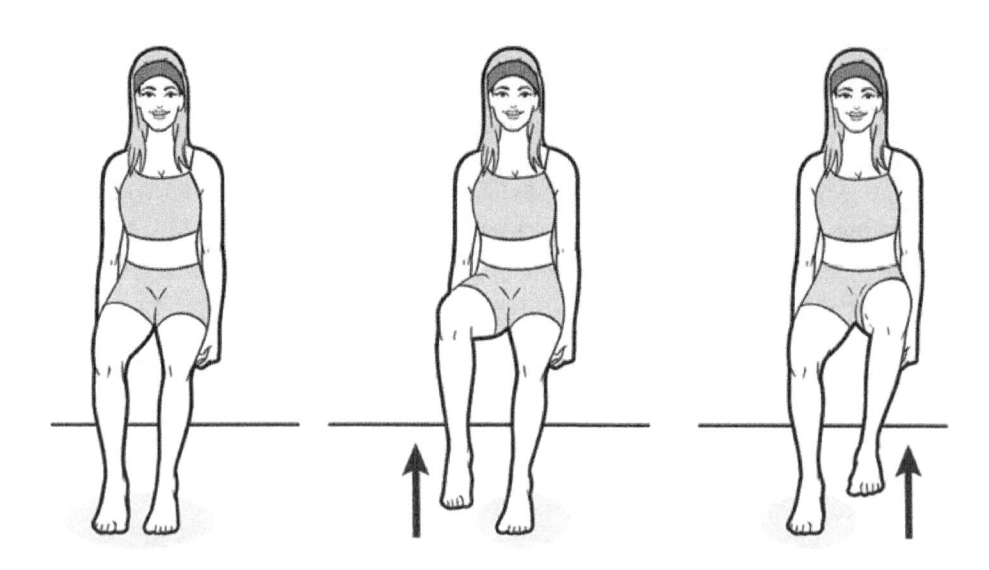

This workout targets leg, hip, and core muscles, aiming to boost strength in the lower body and improve balance and coordination. It emphasizes correct posture and stability throughout the exercise.

Steps
1. Start by standing with your back against the wall, stepping your feet 1-2 feet in front of you.
2. Breathe in, and as you exhale, tighten your core and lower into a half squat by sliding down the wall.
3. Take another breath in. As you breathe out, lift one knee up, then inhale as you lower it back down and switch to lift the other knee, mimicking a marching motion.
4. Keep the movement focused on alternating knee lifts.
5. Ensure your hips stay even, maintain a straight spine against the wall, and keep your abdominal muscles activated for controlled movements.
6. Alternate lifting each knee for 3-5 repetitions, then slide up to return to the standing position. Aim for 2-3 sets of this routine.

Modifications
- For an easier version, reduce the squat depth or lower the height of your knee lifts.
- Adjust the number of sets up or down to suit your desired level of challenge.

Problem Solving and Correction
- Problem: Compromised balance and reduced effectiveness of the exercise in targeting leg and hip muscles due to leaning forward or shifting weight onto your toes.
  - *Correction*: As you lower into the squat and extend your leg, focus on keeping your back in contact with the wall and your weight evenly distributed through your supporting foot, with your heel firmly planted on the ground. Avoid letting your upper body lean forward, or your weight shift onto your toes. If you find yourself leaning or shifting, pause, reset your alignment, and continue the exercise, focusing on maintaining a stable, upright posture.

Wall Squat With Heel Lift

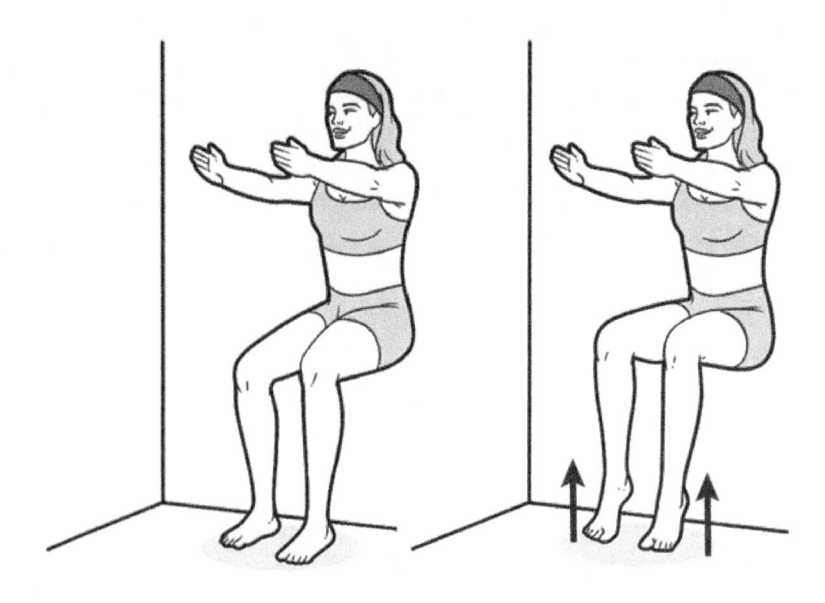

This movement effectively strengthens the quadriceps, hamstrings, glutes, calves, and core, particularly emphasizing the calves. It improves the endurance of the core and lower body, benefiting from the sustained holding position.

Steps
1. Start by standing with your back against the wall and step your feet 1-2 feet forward from it. This spacing will influence the depth of your squat.
2. Take a deep breath in, and as you exhale, engage your core by drawing your navel toward your spine.
3. Slide down the wall into a squat, aiming for your thighs to be either parallel to the floor or entering a half squat for less intensity.
4. Breathe in, and on your next exhale, lift your heels off the ground, shifting your weight onto the balls of your feet. Inhale as you gently lower your heels back down.
5. Maintain focus on engaging your core, breathing effectively, and keeping your spine straight and pressed against the wall.
6. Complete 5-8 heel lift repetitions, then slide upward to return to standing. Aim to do 2-3 sets in total.

Modifications
- The difficulty of this exercise is influenced by how deep you squat.
- To make it more challenging, add more repetitions or perform additional sets.

Problem Solving and Correction

- Problem: Undue stress on your lumbar spine from leaning forward or excessively arching the back.
  - *Correction*: Ensure proper alignment by keeping your back against the wall throughout the exercise. Engage your core muscles to stabilize the spine and pelvis, preventing excessive forward lean or arching of the back. Focus on maintaining an upright posture with the shoulders relaxed and the chest lifted.
- Problem: Reduced effectiveness of the exercise caused by inability to lift heels without losing balance.
  - *Correction*: Start with a smaller range of motion for the heel lift until balance improves. Focus on distributing weight evenly through the feet. Gradually increase the height of the heel lifts as balance and strength progress, ensuring control and stability throughout the movement.
- Problem: Recruitment of incorrect muscles due to knees collapsing inward during Wall Squat With Heel Lift.
  - *Correction*: Pay attention to knee alignment by tracking it directly over the second toe throughout the squatting motion. Engage the muscles of the outer thighs and hips to help prevent an inward collapse of the knee. Focus on spreading the floor apart with the feet to maintain proper alignment and stability in the lower body.

Bridge

The Bridge exercise effectively targets the glutes, hamstrings, and lower back, enhancing strength and stability throughout the posterior chain. This exercise is particularly beneficial for individuals who spend extensive periods sitting for work, as it can alleviate various types of back pain.

Steps
1. Start by lying on your mat with your back flat, positioning yourself so that your feet are against the wall and knees bent at a 90-degree angle.
2. Take a deep breath in, and then, as you exhale, engage your core by drawing your navel toward your spine. Lift your hips off the floor into a bridge position by rolling your spine off the mat and pressing your feet firmly against the wall.
3. While holding the bridge position, inhale, ensuring your abdominal muscles remain tight. Then, exhale slowly as you carefully roll your spine back down to the mat, lowering your hips last.
4. Aim to pull your shoulders down toward your heels and press your shoulder blades into the floor for added stability.
5. Keep your core engaged throughout the exercise.
6. Execute 8-15 repetitions of the bridge lift, focusing on slow, controlled movements.

Modifications
- For an easier version, lift your hips less high off the floor during the bridge.
- To make the exercise more challenging, either perform more repetitions or add an additional set.

Problem Solving and Correction

- Problem: Feeling discomfort or strain in the neck or shoulders due to overstretching your neck.
    - *Correction*: Ensure proper head and neck alignment by gently tucking the chin toward the chest, avoiding any tension in the neck muscles. Additionally, distribute weight evenly across the shoulders and upper back, and avoid shrugging the shoulders toward the ears. Relax your neck and shoulders to lift the hips while engaging the glutes and hamstrings.
- Problem: Lack of engagement in the glutes or hamstrings causing reduced spinal stability during the Bridge.
    - *Correction*: Concentrate on squeezing the glutes at the top of the bridge movement and actively pressing through the heels to engage the hamstrings. Focus on maintaining tension in the posterior chain throughout the exercise by visualizing lifting the hips toward the ceiling while keeping the knees aligned with the ankles.

Bridge With Knee Lift

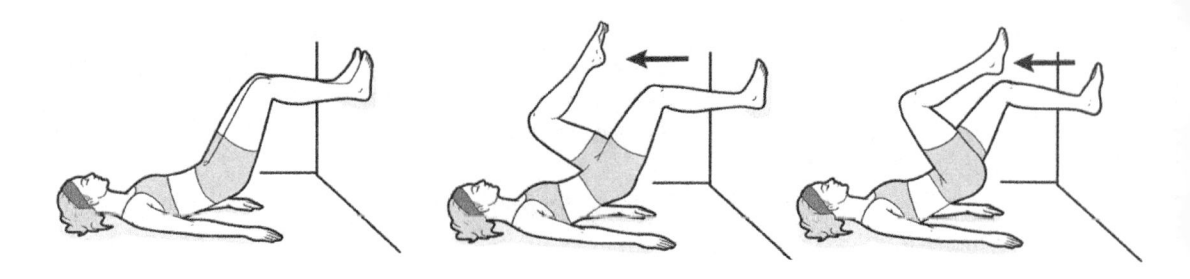

This exercise strengthens the glutes, hamstrings, and core, focusing on stability and strength. It includes a knee lift to engage the hip flexors further, intensifying the workout. This move not only fortifies the hip and core muscles but also puts the pelvic and spinal stability to the test.

Steps
1. Start by lying on your mat with your back flat, positioning yourself so your feet can press flat against the wall and your knees are bent at about 90 degrees.
2. Take a deep breath in. As you breathe out, engage your core by drawing your navel toward your spine. Roll your spine off the mat to lift your hips into a bridge position, pressing your feet against the wall.
3. Inhale, then, as you exhale, lift one knee by raising your foot off the wall, bending at the hip. Inhale as you return that foot to the wall. Exhale and alternate with the other leg, mimicking a marching motion while maintaining the bridge.
4. Concentrate on keeping your hips and pelvis steady, your core engaged, and executing the movement with controlled, deliberate motions.
5. Aim to do 3-5 knee lifts on each side per set, completing 2-3 sets in total.

Modifications
- For a less challenging version, make the movements smaller.
- To increase the intensity, add more repetitions or sets or hold each lift for a longer period.

Problem Solving and Correction
- Problem: Difficulty maintaining balance or stability during the Bridge With Knee Lift.
  - *Correction*: Focus on stabilizing through the supporting foot and engaging the core muscles to maintain balance. Ensure proper alignment of the hips and shoulders throughout the movement, and keep the movement controlled to prevent wobbling or tipping to one side.
- Problem: Feeling strain or discomfort in the lower back caused by excessive arching or rounding of the lower back.
  - *Correction*: Prioritize maintaining a neutral spine by engaging the core muscles and avoiding excessive arching or rounding of the lower back. Focus on pressing through

the heels and lifting the hips toward the ceiling while keeping the spine lengthened, alleviating strain on the lower back.
- Problem: Inadequate activation of the glutes or hamstrings during the knee lift, putting undue stress on your lower back and spine.
  - *Correction*: Concentrate on squeezing the glutes and engaging the hamstrings as you lift the knee toward the chest. Ensure that the movement is initiated from the hip, rather than solely relying on momentum from the knee lift, to effectively target the intended muscle groups.

Bridge With Straight Leg Lift

This challenging workout targets the glutes, hamstrings, and core, adding a straight leg lift to increase hip strength. It rigorously works the core, hips, and legs, blending strength and endurance training with a focus on maintaining pelvic stability.

Steps
1. Start by lying on your mat with your back flat, positioning your glutes and feet so you can place your feet flat against the wall.
2. Ensure your position allows you to extend your legs up the wall, straightening your knees.
3. Breathe in, then as you exhale, engage your core by drawing your navel toward your spine. Lift your hips off the floor into a bridge position, pressing your feet against the wall.
4. Inhale again, then lift one leg away from the wall, keeping your knee straight as you exhale. Inhale as you gently return your leg to the wall.

5. Follow the same breathing pattern as you switch legs, lifting the other leg straight up, then exhaling and lowering it back to the wall.
6. Keep your core tight and ensure your hips and pelvis remain level throughout the exercise.
7. Perform 8-10 lifts for each leg per set, aiming for 2-3 sets in total.

Modifications

- For an easier version, keep your knees slightly bent during the leg lifts and avoid lifting your hips too high off the ground.
- To increase the intensity, add more repetitions to each set or include additional sets to your workout.

Problem Solving and Correction

- Problem: Difficulty maintaining stability or balance during the straight leg lift, causing undue stress on your lower back.
  - *Correction*: Focus on stabilizing through the supporting foot and engaging the core muscles to maintain balance. Ensure proper alignment of the hips and shoulders throughout the movement, and keep the movement controlled to prevent wobbling or tipping to one side.
- Problem: Insufficient activation of the glutes or hamstrings during the straight leg lift, making the exercise less safe.
  - *Correction*: Concentrate on squeezing the glutes and engaging the hamstrings as you lift your leg. Ensure that the movement is initiated from the hip, rather than solely relying on momentum from the leg lift, to effectively target the intended muscle groups.

Wall Scissors

This exercise focuses on the abdominals, hip flexors, and inner thighs, using the wall for stability and support. It strengthens the legs, hips, and core while also enhancing hip mobility and increasing flexibility in the groin area.

Steps
1. Start by lying on your back with your buttocks touching the wall and your legs extended upward along the wall. Spread your arms out to the sides on the floor to form a T shape.
2. Breathe in, then as you breathe out, engage your core by drawing your navel toward your spine. Lower your legs outward in a straddle position while inhaling, and bring them back together as you exhale.
3. Continue this pattern: inhale as you open your legs and exhale as you close them.
4. Keep your spine pressed firmly against the floor, synchronize your breathing with each movement of your legs, and maintain core engagement throughout the exercise.
5. Aim to complete 10-15 repetitions of the scissors movement.

Modifications
- For a less intense workout, reduce the distance you move your legs outward.
- To increase the intensity, move your legs more slowly and concentrate on contracting the inner thigh muscles for a more profound effect.

Problem Solving and Correction

- Problem: Difficulty maintaining control and stability during the wall scissors exercise, putting your spine at risk of injury.
  - *Correction*: Focus on engaging the core muscles to stabilize the pelvis and spine throughout the movement. Ensure proper alignment of the shoulders and hips against the wall and maintain a slight posterior pelvic tilt to prevent excessive lower back arching. Perform the movement slowly and with control, avoiding jerky or unsteady motions.
- Problem: Limited range of motion or flexibility in the legs.
  - *Correction*: Start with a smaller range of motion for the leg movements, focusing on maintaining proper alignment and control. Gradually increase the range of motion as flexibility improves, but only go as far as possible while maintaining control and stability. Use a strap or towel around the foot of the lifted leg if necessary to assist with reaching the desired range of motion.

Bridge With Knee to Chest

This exercise strengthens the glutes, hamstrings, and abdominals, featuring a knee-to-chest movement to boost core strength and hip flexibility. It also focuses on improving pelvic and spinal stability, as well as mobility in the hips and knees.

Steps
1. Start by lying on your mat with your back flat, positioning your glutes and feet so that your feet rest flat against the wall. Ensure your glutes are about 10-12 inches away from the wall, allowing room to slide your legs up the wall.
2. Breathe in, then as you exhale, engage your core by drawing your navel toward your spine.
3. Lift your hips off the mat into a bridge position, pressing both feet against the wall.
4. Inhale, then lift one leg from the wall, drawing your knee toward your chest as you exhale.
5. Inhale as you extend the leg back out, maintaining the bridge position. Focus on this leg movement while keeping the bridge position stable.
6. Maintain core engagement, ensure your body remains straight, and keep your pelvis and hips even.
7. Perform 8-10 repetitions for each leg, alternating legs, before gently lowering your hips back to the mat.

Modifications
- Given its difficulty, it's advisable to attempt this exercise after gaining some experience with Pilates.
- To make it easier, lower the height of your bridge, reduce the number of repetitions, and keep your knees slightly bent.
- For an increased challenge, add more repetitions or include an additional set.

Problem Solving and Correction

- Problem: Difficulty maintaining stability or balance during the bridge with knee-to-chest movement.
  - ***Correction***: Focus on stabilizing through the supporting foot and engaging the core muscles to maintain balance. Ensure proper alignment of the hips and shoulders throughout the movement, and keep the movement controlled to prevent wobbling or tipping to one side.

Bridge With Knee Circles

This exercise targets the glutes, hamstrings, and core with knee circles to improve hip mobility and stability. It effectively strengthens the hips, legs, and core, combining endurance training with exercises for hip flexibility and pelvic stability.

Steps
1. Start by lying on your mat with your back down, positioning yourself so that when your feet are flat against the wall, your knees form 90-degree angles.
2. Take a deep breath in. As you breathe out, engage your core, lift your hips into a bridge position by rolling your spine off the mat, and press your feet against the wall.
3. Inhale as you draw one knee halfway toward your chest. Exhale and initiate a circular motion with your hip, keeping the knee bent, to complete half of the circle.
4. Continue to breathe in and out with each semicircular movement.
5. Execute 8-10 circles with one leg, both clockwise and counterclockwise, then gently lower your hips to the mat to rest before switching legs.
6. Maintain a steady pelvis and an engaged core, ensuring the circular motions are smooth and controlled.

Modifications
- Given its difficulty, master keeping your hips stable during this exercise before incorporating it into your routine regularly.
- To make it easier, reduce the number of repetitions or lower the height of your bridge.
- For a greater challenge, increase the number of repetitions or add an extra set.

Problem Solving and Correction
- Problem: Feeling strain or discomfort in the lower back caused by excessive arching or rounding of the lower back.

- *Correction*: Prioritize maintaining a neutral spine position by engaging your core and avoiding excessive arching or rounding of the lower back. Focus on pressing through the heels and lifting the hips toward the ceiling while keeping the spine lengthened, alleviating strain on the lower back.
- Problem: Inadequate activation of the glutes or hamstrings during the knee circles, putting undue stress on the lower back.
  - *Correction*: Concentrate on squeezing the glutes and engaging the hamstrings throughout the movement. Ensure that the movement of the knees is controlled and initiated from the hip, rather than relying solely on momentum from the leg movement, to effectively target the intended muscle groups.

Kneeling With Side Leg Kick

This dynamic wall Pilates exercise, performed while kneeling, aims at the outer thighs, hips, and core, designed to boost stability and balance. It emphasizes maintaining pelvic stability and demands adequate hip mobility for effective execution.

Steps
1. Start by kneeling upright close to the wall, with one hip and shoulder near it.
1. Place your forearm on the wall for support and extend the leg farthest from the wall out to the side, forming a right angle with your body.
2. Breathe in, then as you exhale, lift the extended leg upward.
3. Inhale again as you gently lower the leg back to the starting position. Follow this breathing pattern for each repetition.
4. Keep your upper body steady, ensure your core is activated, and move your leg with precision.
5. Complete 10-15 raises with this leg, then switch sides by turning around and repeating the exercise with the other leg.

Modifications
- For an easier version, lift your leg to a lower height, slightly bend the knee, or reduce the number of repetitions.
- To increase the difficulty, add an extra set or perform more repetitions.

Problem Solving and Correction
- Problem: Difficulty maintaining proper alignment and stability while kneeling.
  - *Correction*: Focus on stabilizing through the supporting knee and engaging the core muscles to maintain balance. Ensure proper alignment of the shoulders, hips, and

knees throughout the movement, and keep the movement controlled to prevent leaning or shifting to one side.

Kneeling Pendulum Kick

This exercise, done from a kneeling position, activates the hip abductors and core stabilizers, focusing on improving balance and control. Pendulum kicks put your pelvic and spinal stability to the test while strengthening the muscles in your hips, legs, and core.

Steps
1. Start in a tall-kneeling position close to the wall, with one hip and shoulder near it.
2. Place your hand on the wall, extend your arm, and stretch the opposite leg directly out to the side.
3. Breathe in, then as you exhale, tighten your core. Lift the extended leg off the ground on your next inhale.
4. Exhale as you swing the extended leg forward, and inhale as you move it back, synchronizing the movements of your outstretched arm with your leg, reaching forward and back.
5. Maintain controlled leg movements, swinging forward and backward without touching the floor, ensuring your core remains activated throughout.
6. Execute the pendulum kick motion 5-8 times before placing your leg down. Afterward, switch sides by turning your body and repeating with the opposite leg.

Modifications
- For a less challenging version, lean on your forearm, swing the leg at a lower height, or bend the knee slightly.
- To intensify the exercise, perform more repetitions or add an extra set.

Problem Solving and Correction
- Problem: Limited range of motion or flexibility in the hip, meaning you cannot reach far forward or backward.
  - *Correction*: Start with a smaller range of motion for the pendulum kick and gradually

increase it as flexibility improves. Focus on moving the leg with control and stability, ensuring the movement originates from the hip joint. Incorporate hip mobility exercises into your routine to improve your range of motion over time.

Kneeling Side Leg Circles

This exercise, conducted from a kneeling position, focuses on the outer thighs and hips. It involves deliberate circular leg movements to improve hip flexibility and strengthen the abductor muscles. In addition to enhancing hip mobility, it bolsters the muscles in the hips, legs, and core, promoting both pelvic and spinal stability.

Steps
1. Start by kneeling upright near the wall, with one hip and shoulder close to it. Place your forearm on the wall for support.
2. Lift the leg farthest from the wall, exhaling as you begin.
3. Inhale while you move the leg in a backward circle, and exhale as you complete the circle.
4. Keep the leg raised off the floor throughout.
5. Do 5-8 circles in a backward direction, then switch to perform the same number of circles in a forward direction with the same leg.
6. Ensure your upper body remains stationary, your core is tight, and you're controlling the movement of your leg circles smoothly.
7. After completing the set, switch sides and repeat the exercise with the other leg.

Modifications
- For an easier variation, keep your leg closer to the ground and make smaller circles.
- To increase the challenge, enlarge the circles and execute them more slowly.

Problem Solving and Correction
- Problem: Difficulty maintaining stability or balance during kneeling side leg circles, putting yourself at risk of falling over or back strain.
  - *Correction*: Focus on stabilizing through the supporting knee and engaging the core muscles to maintain balance. Ensure proper alignment of the shoulders, hips, and knees throughout the movement, and keep the movement controlled to prevent swaying or tipping to one side.
- Problem: Feeling strain or discomfort in the lower back due to excessive rounding or

arching.
- ***Correction***: Prioritize maintaining a neutral spine position by engaging the core muscles and avoiding excessive arching or rounding of the lower back. Focus on keeping the torso upright and stable while performing the leg circles, alleviating strain on the lower back.

CORE

Single Knee Stretch

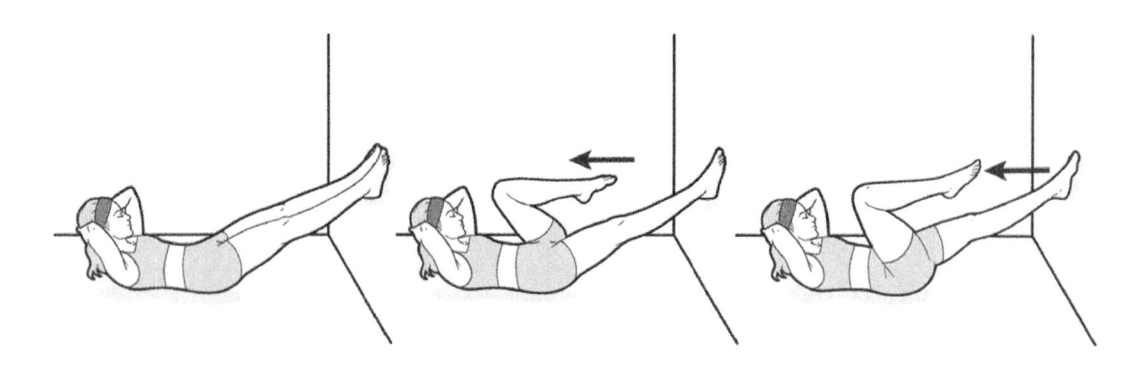

This core-focused exercise works the abdominals and hip flexors from a lying down position, alternating knee-to-chest movements to improve core strength and stability. It requires significant control, emphasizing slow, deliberate knee movements to ensure each motion is precise and effective.

Steps
1. Start by lying on your back on the mat, positioning your feet toward the wall.
2. Press your legs against the wall to extend them fully, and place your hands behind your head for support.
3. Take a deep breath in, and as you exhale, tighten your core, lifting your head but keeping a gap between your chin and chest. Inhale again.
4. While exhaling, draw one knee toward your chest. Inhale as you extend that leg back against the wall.
5. On your next exhale, bring the opposite knee in toward your chest.
6. Continue to alternate legs, performing 8-10 repetitions in total, then gently rest your head back on the mat.
7. Maintain core engagement and steady breathing as you alternate legs, ensuring the non-moving leg remains pressed against the wall, and your spine is flat on the mat.

Modifications
- To make the exercise more challenging, increase the number of repetitions or add an additional set.

Problem Solving and Correction
- Problem: Difficulty maintaining proper form and control during the single knee stretch.
  - *Correction*: Focus on engaging the core muscles throughout the exercise to stabilize the pelvis and spine. Ensure proper alignment of the shoulders, hips, and knees, and

keep the movement controlled and deliberate to prevent momentum from taking over.
- Problem: Shrugging the shoulders toward the ears causing strain or discomfort in the neck or shoulders.
  - *Correction*: Relax the shoulders and neck, ensuring they remain comfortable and neutral throughout the exercise. Avoid shrugging the shoulders or tensing the neck muscles. Engage the upper back muscles to support the shoulders and maintain stability.

Single Straight Leg Stretch

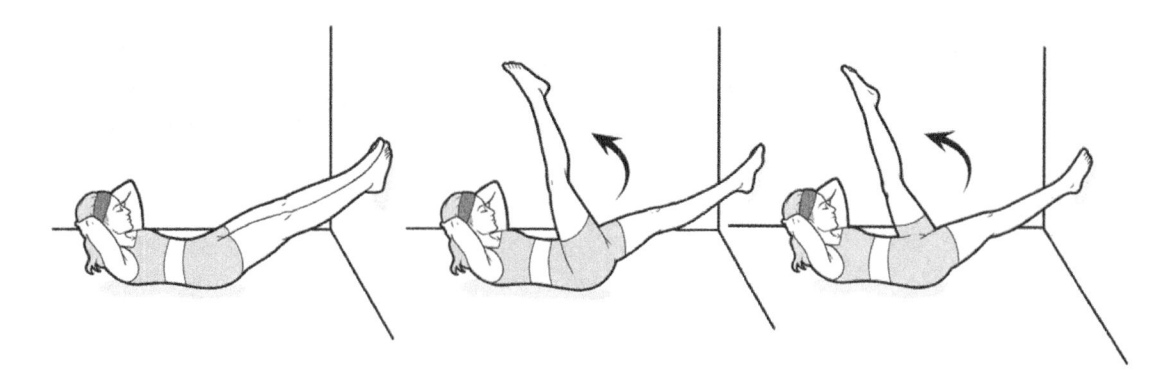

This exercise deepens core engagement, targeting the abdominals and hip flexors. Building on the Single Knee Stretch, it presents a more advanced challenge by extending one leg straight out, demanding greater control over the extended limb.

Steps
1. Start by lying on your back on the mat with your legs facing toward the wall.
2. Press your feet against the wall to straighten your legs, and place your hands above your head for support.
3. Breathe in, and as you breathe out, activate your core, lifting your head but maintaining a gap between your chin and chest. Inhale again.
4. While exhaling, raise one leg away from the wall, keeping it straight.
5. Inhale as you place that leg back against the wall.
6. Exhale while lifting the alternate leg in a straight position off the wall.
7. Continue alternating legs for a total of 8-10 repetitions, then gently rest your head back on the mat.
8. Throughout the exercise, ensure your core remains engaged, and your breathing is consistent, with the non-moving leg pressing against the wall and your spine flat on the mat.

Modifications
- To make the exercise easier, keep your head on the mat while performing the leg movements.
- For a greater challenge, increase the number of repetitions or add an extra set.

Problem Solving and Correction
- Problem: Difficulty maintaining proper form and control during the single straight leg stretch, putting yourself at risk of back injury or strain.
  - *Correction*: Focus on engaging the core muscles throughout the exercise to stabilize the pelvis and spine. Ensure proper alignment of the shoulders, hips, and legs, and

keep the movement controlled and deliberate to prevent strain or injury.

Cross Over

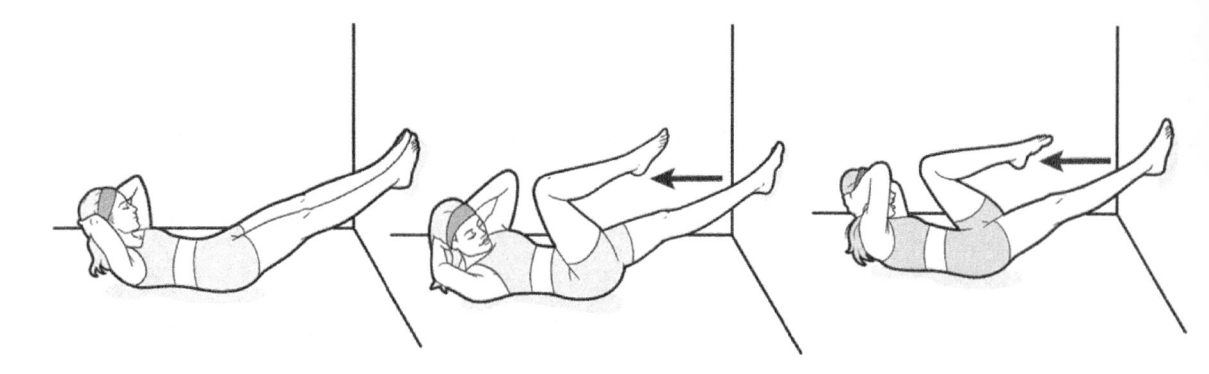

This wall Pilates move focuses on the obliques, hip flexors, and abdominals. It's a variation of the Single Knee Stretch that offers a tougher workout for the obliques by incorporating a deeper crunch and a slight rotational twist of the torso.

Steps
1. Start by lying on your back on the mat with your legs facing the wall.
2. Press your feet against the wall to extend your legs, placing your hands behind your head for support.
3. Breathe in, then as you exhale, tighten your core and lift your head, creating a gap between your chin and chest.
4. Inhale, and as you exhale, draw one knee toward your chest while rotating your torso so your opposite elbow moves toward the knee, mimicking a bicycle crunch motion.
5. Inhale as you extend that leg back against the wall, then exhale and repeat the movement with the other knee and elbow, rotating in the opposite direction.
6. Alternate this motion for 8-10 repetitions, then gently rest your head back on the mat to finish.
7. Throughout the exercise, maintain core engagement and steady breathing, ensuring the non-moving leg presses against the wall, and your spine stays imprinted on the mat.

Modifications
- For an easier version, reduce the range of your leg movement and keep your head closer to the mat, minimizing torso rotation.
- To make the exercise more challenging, increase the number of repetitions or add an extra set.

Problem Solving and Correction
- Problem: Feeling strain or discomfort in the lower back due to maintaining a non-neutral spine position.

- *Correction*: Prioritize maintaining a neutral spine position by engaging the core muscles and avoiding excessive arching or rounding of the lower back. Focus on pressing the lower back into the mat while performing the leg movements to alleviate strain on the lower back.
- Problem: Inadequate engagement of the obliques while performing the exercise.
    - *Correction*: Concentrate on initiating the movement from the obliques by actively bringing one knee toward the opposite shoulder while keeping the other leg stable. Focus on twisting from the waist and maintaining tension in the oblique muscles throughout the exercise.

Hands on Wall Toe Taps

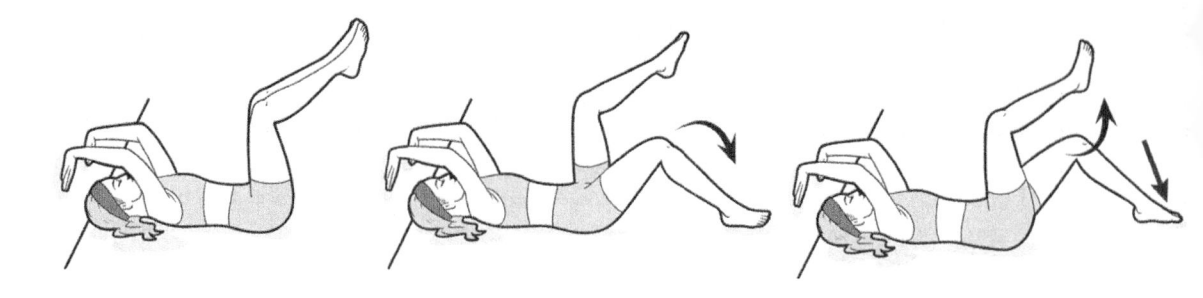

This exercise strengthens the core by engaging the abdominals and hip flexors but also involves a wide range of muscles, including those in the arms, shoulders, and legs. While some muscles perform the movement, others help stabilize the body. It's a mild core workout, making it ideal for beginners.

Steps
1. Start by lying on your back on the mat, positioning your head near the wall.
2. Extend your arms above your head with your hands pressing against the wall, fingers pointing down, and elbows positioned just above your shoulders.
3. Press firmly into the wall with your hands and draw your shoulder blades down toward your ribcage.
4. Flatten your spine against the mat, take a deep breath in, and activate your core muscles as you exhale and lift both legs to a table-top position (knees bent at a 90-degree angle and thighs perpendicular to the floor).
5. Inhale, then exhale and lower one leg toward the floor, bending at the knee.
6. Lightly tap the floor with your toes, inhale, and as you exhale, return the leg to the table-top position.
7. Switch legs and repeat the motion.
8. Keep your spine pressed into the mat, maintain pressure with your hands against the wall, engage your core, and ensure your breathing is controlled and rhythmic.
9. Perform this leg alternating movement for 8-10 repetitions.

Modifications
- To simplify the exercise, reduce the range of your leg movement by not tapping the floor with your toes.
- To intensify the workout, perform additional repetitions or include an extra set.

Problem Solving and Correction
- Problem: Inadequate engagement of the abdominals or hip flexors reducing the effectiveness of the exercise.
  - **Correction**: Concentrate on actively drawing the navel toward the spine to engage the deep core muscles. Focus on initiating the movement from the core rather than

relying solely on momentum. Ensure the hip flexors are also engaged by lifting the legs with control and stability.

Hands on Wall Both Legs Lower

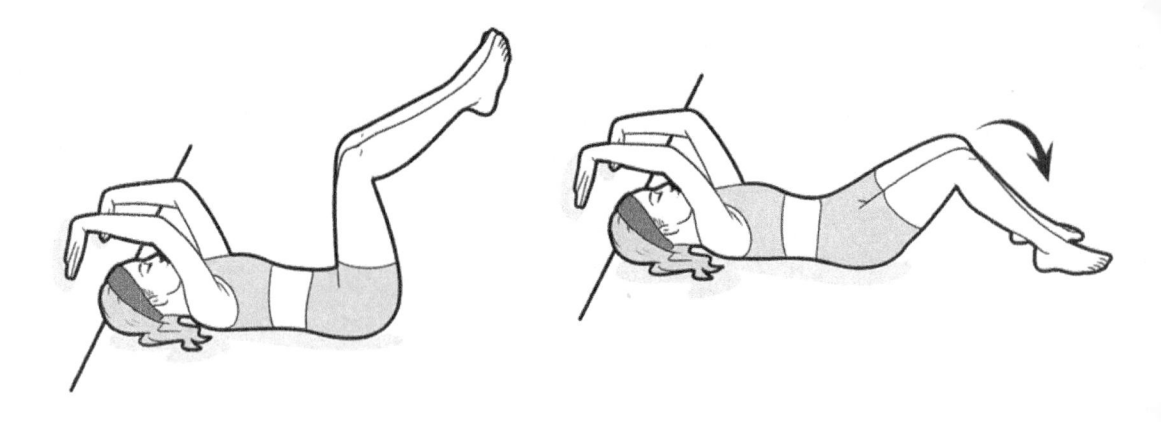

This exercise, like the Hands on Wall Toe Taps, targets the core, specifically the abdominal muscles and hip flexors, but also engages a wide array of muscles, including those in the arms, shoulders, and legs. While some muscles are actively involved in the movement, others play a key role in stabilization.

Steps
1. Lie on your back on the mat with your head near the wall.
2. Reach your hands above your head to press against the wall, fingers pointing toward the floor, and position your elbows just above your shoulders.
3. Press into the wall with your hands and draw your shoulder blades down toward your ribcage.
4. Flatten your spine against the mat, take a deep breath in, and as you breathe out, activate your core, lifting both legs to a table-top position.
5. Inhale again, and on your next exhale, slowly lower both legs toward the floor, keeping your knees slightly bent.
6. Lightly tap the floor with your toes, then inhale and use your exhale to raise your legs back to the table-top position.
7. Keep your spine pressed firmly against the mat, maintain pressure with your hands against the wall, ensure your core is active, and breathe consistently.
8. Complete 5-10 repetitions of lowering and lifting your legs.

Modifications
- For an easier variation, reduce the distance you lower your legs, avoiding touching the floor with your toes.
- To make the exercise more challenging, increase the number of repetitions or add an additional set.

Problem Solving and Correction

- Problem: Undue stress on the lower back due to an inability to lower both legs without compensating with the lower back.
  - *Correction*: Start with a smaller range of motion for the leg lowering movement and gradually increase it as core strength and control improve. Focus on maintaining stability through the core and pelvis throughout the movement, and lower the legs as far as you can while keeping the lower back flat against the ground.

Hands on Wall Single Leg Stretch

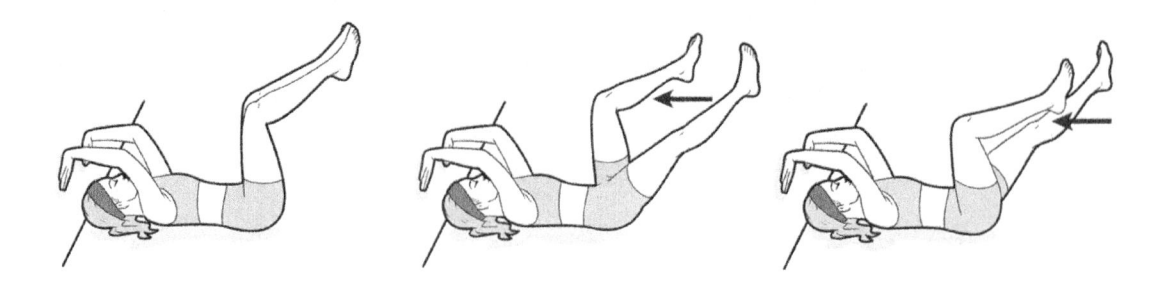

This exercise targets the core, specifically the abdominals, obliques, and hip flexors, offering a higher difficulty level among the 'Hands on Wall' core exercises. The key challenge is maintaining core engagement to prevent your lower back from lifting off the ground. It also enhances hip mobility and leg flexibility.

Steps
1. Lie on your back on the mat with your head near the wall.
2. Extend your arms overhead, placing your hands on the wall with fingers pointing toward the floor and elbows slightly above your shoulders.
3. Press firmly against the wall with your hands and draw your shoulder blades down toward your ribcage.
4. Press your spine against the mat, take a deep breath in, and as you breathe out, activate your core, lifting both legs to a table-top position.
5. While keeping one leg in the table-top position, straighten the other leg out in front of you.
6. Maintain focus on keeping your spine pressed against the mat, your hands pressing into the wall, your core engaged, and your breathing controlled.
7. Alternate extending each leg for 8-10 repetitions.

Modifications
- For an easier version, you don't need to extend your leg fully.
- To intensify the workout, extend the leg closer to the floor and either increase the number of repetitions or add an extra set.

Problem Solving and Correction
- Problem: Excessive arching or rounding causing strain or discomfort in the lower back.
  - *Correction*: Prioritize maintaining a neutral spine position by engaging the core muscles and avoiding excessive arching or rounding of the lower back. Focus on pressing the lower back into the ground and maintaining tension in the abdominals while performing the leg movements, alleviating strain on the lower back.
- Problem: Inability to extend the leg fully without compromising form.
  - *Correction*: Start with a smaller range of motion for the leg extension and gradually

increase it as core strength and control improve. Focus on maintaining stability through the core and pelvis throughout the movement, and only extend the leg as far as you can while keeping the lower back flat against the ground.

Hands on Wall Double Leg Stretch

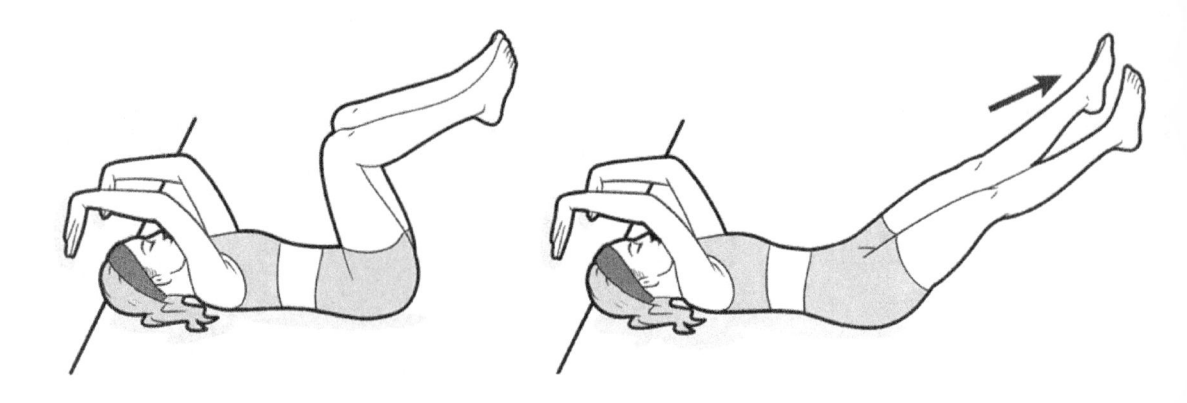

This exercise builds on the Hands on Wall Single Leg Stretch by targeting the abdominals and hip flexors. Additionally, it engages the quadriceps, glutes, lower back, and shoulders. As a more advanced version, it presents a significant challenge in keeping your lower back firmly against the ground while performing the movement. If maintaining this contact proves difficult, continue with the Single Leg Stretch until you're ready to advance.

Steps
1. Start by lying on your back on the mat, positioning your head near the wall.
2. Reach your arms overhead to place your hands on the wall, with fingers pointing toward the floor and elbows positioned slightly above your shoulders.
3. Press your hands against the wall and draw your shoulder blades down toward your ribcage.
4. Press your spine against the mat, take a deep breath in, and as you exhale, activate your core, lifting both legs to a table-top position.
5. Take another breath in, then as you exhale, stretch both legs out straight in front of you at a 45-degree angle from the floor.
6. Inhale as you bring your legs back to the table-top position.
7. Maintain focus on pressing your spine into the mat, keeping your hands pressed against the wall, engaging your core, and controlling your breath.
8. Complete 5-10 repetitions of extending both legs out and then returning them to the table-top position.

Modifications
- For a simpler version, reduce the range of the leg extension or lessen the distance you lower your legs.
- To add difficulty, lower your legs closer to the floor and either increase the number of repetitions or include an extra set.

Problem Solving and Correction

- Problem: Inability to fully extend both legs without compromising form during the Hands on Wall Double Leg Stretch.
    - *Correction*: Start with a smaller range of motion for the leg movement and gradually increase it as core strength and control improve. Focus on maintaining stability through the core and pelvis throughout the movement, and only extend the legs as far as you can while keeping the lower back flat against the ground.

Hands on Wall Scissors

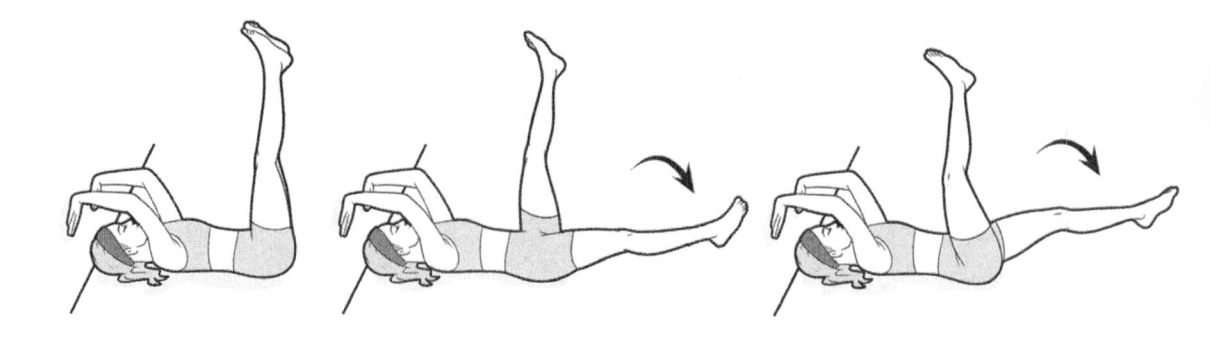

In this 'Hands on Wall' exercise variation, you'll experience a more intense stretch in the abdominals, obliques, and hip flexors. Lowering your legs closer to the floor intensifies the workout for these muscles, requiring greater control to execute properly.

Steps
1. Lie on your back on the mat with your head near the wall, extending your arms overhead to place your hands on the wall, fingers pointing toward the floor, and elbows slightly above your shoulders.
2. Press against the wall with your hands and draw your shoulder blades toward your ribcage.
3. Press your spine against the mat, take a deep breath in, and as you exhale, activate your core, raising both legs to a table-top position.
4. Inhale as you extend both legs upward, then exhale and separate your legs in a scissor motion: keep one leg still while extending the other away, keeping both legs straight.
5. Continue inhaling and exhaling smoothly as you switch legs in this scissor motion, maintaining engagement of your core throughout.
6. Keep your spine pressed firmly against the mat, your hands pushing into the wall, your core tight, and ensure your breathing is consistent.
7. Complete 8-10 repetitions of this scissor motion, alternating the straight leg movements.

Modifications
- Reduce the range of the scissor motion to make the exercise easier.
- To heighten the intensity, perform additional repetitions or add an extra set.

Problem Solving and Correction
- Problem: Inability to fully extend both legs without compromising form, causing undue stress on the lower back.
    - *Correction*: Start with a smaller range of motion for the leg movement and gradually

increase it as core strength and control improve. Focus on maintaining stability through the core and pelvis throughout the movement, and only extend the legs as far as you can while keeping your lower back flat against the ground.
- Problem: Experiencing strain or discomfort in the shoulders or arms due to misalignment of positioning.
  - ***Correction***: Ensure proper alignment of the shoulders and distribute weight evenly through the hands pressing against the wall. Avoid shrugging your shoulders and maintain a slight bend in the elbows to reduce strain on the arms. Focus on engaging the upper back muscles to support the shoulders and maintain stability.

Feet at Wall "The Hundred"

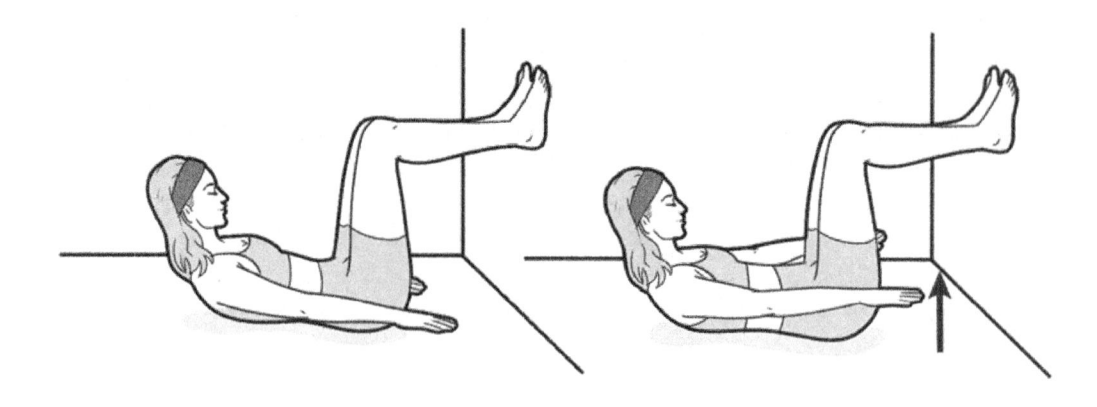

"The Hundred" is a renowned Pilates exercise that improves core strength and endurance. This exercise demands synchronized breath and movement, aiming for strength and fluidity. It activates the abdominal muscles, including the obliques, and requires stability in the scapula and torso.

Steps
1. Start by lying on your back on the mat with your feet aimed at the wall and positioned so you can press your feet against the wall, knees bent at a 90-degree angle.
2. Lift your head and shoulders off the mat, extend your arms toward your feet, and draw your navel in toward your spine.
3. Engage in a rapid, controlled arm movement, moving your arms up and down as though lightly tapping a table's surface.
4. Your breathing rhythm should be approximately 5 arm taps for every inhale and exhale cycle.
5. Complete this exercise in 10 sets, with each set consisting of 5 cycles of inhaling and exhaling.
6. Concentrate on steady breathing, precise arm motions, engaging your core muscles, and maintaining a gap between your chin and chest.

Modifications
- For a less intense version, keep your head on the mat and divide the sets as necessary to make the exercise more manageable.

Problem Solving and Correction
- Problem: Difficulty maintaining stability or control during Feet At Wall "The Hundred."
  - **Correction**: Focus on stabilizing through the core muscles, ensuring proper alignment of the shoulders, hips, and legs against the wall. Keep the movement controlled and avoid overarching or rounding of the lower back to maintain stability throughout the exercise.
- Problem: Feeling strain or discomfort in the lower back caused by arching the lower back

off the ground.
- *Correction*: Prioritize maintaining a neutral spine position by engaging the core muscles and avoiding excessive arching or rounding of the lower back. Press the lower back gently into the ground to support the spine and alleviate strain during the exercise.

Feet at Wall Pendulum Kick

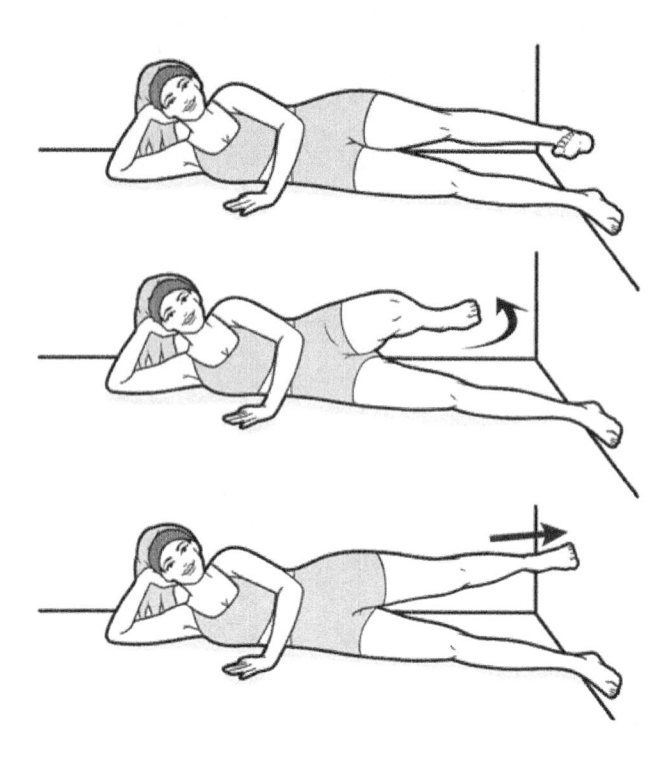

This exercise targets the core, including the abdominals, hip flexors, quadriceps, glutes, and lower back, through a dynamic movement. As a unilateral exercise, it also involves the hip abductors, as you lift and swing your leg away from your body in a forward and backward motion.

Steps
1. Start by lying on your side, aligning yourself perpendicular to the wall, with the bottom foot flat against the wall and positioned slightly ahead of your body.
2. Use your elbow or hand to prop up your head or neck for support. Use your other arm for stability by pressing it into the floor in front of you.
3. Lift your upper leg, keeping the knee straight, and execute a forward and backward kick in a smooth, controlled, pendulum-like motion.
4. Inhale as you move your leg backward, and exhale as you move your leg forward, ensuring your core remains tight.
5. Concentrate on keeping your torso stationary as you perform the leg swings.
6. Complete 8-10 kicks in this pendulum motion before switching sides to ensure both legs are worked evenly.

Modifications
- For an easier variation, reduce the range of the leg swing, bend the knee slightly, or lay your head on the mat.
- To add difficulty, perform more repetitions or include an extra set.

Problem Solving and Correction

- Problem: Maintaining a non-neutral spine during the exercise causing strain or discomfort in the lower back.
  - *Correction*: Prioritize maintaining a neutral spine position by engaging the core muscles and avoiding excessive arching or rounding of the lower back. Press the lower back gently into the ground to support the spine and alleviate strain during the exercise.
- Problem: Inability to fully extend the legs against the wall without compromising form.
  - *Correction*: Start with a smaller range of motion for the leg movement and gradually increase it as flexibility and core strength improve. Focus on maintaining stability through the core and pelvis throughout the movement, ensuring that the lower back remains flat against the ground.

Feet at Wall Side Kick

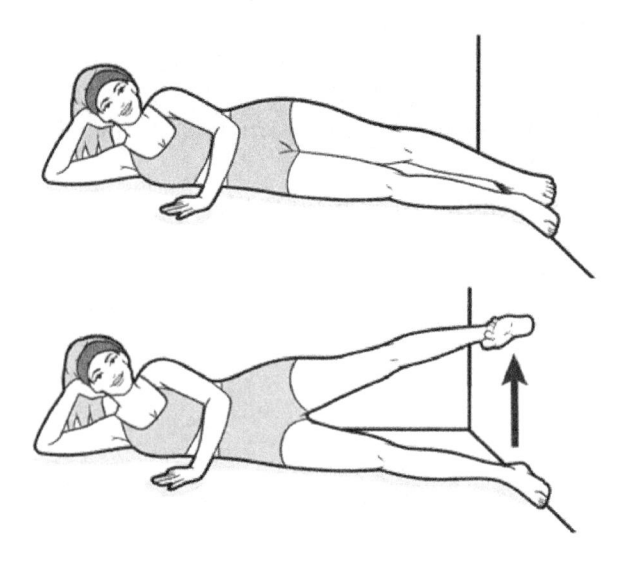

This exercise focuses on strengthening the core, especially targeting the abdominals and obliques. It also involves the hip abductors by lifting the top leg. Emphasizing controlled, slow movements is crucial to prevent strain on the lower back.

Steps
1. Start by lying on one side, with your head turned away from the wall, and place the foot closest to the wall flat against it, slightly ahead of your torso.
2. Use your elbow or hand to support your head and press the other arm onto the floor in front of you for stability.
3. Inhale and then lift your upper leg straight toward the ceiling as you exhale, keeping the leg extended and your body still.
4. Ensure the lower leg remains pressed firmly against the wall.
5. Breathe in and out with each lift of your leg, actively engaging your core muscles throughout the movement.
6. Concentrate on maintaining your hips aligned, one directly over the other.
7. Execute 15-20 kicks with the first leg before switching sides to ensure both legs receive equal training.

Modifications
- Bend the knee slightly or keep the lifts lower for a less intense workout.
- To increase the difficulty, incorporate an additional set or use a resistance band around your ankles.

Problem Solving and Correction
- Problem: Difficulty maintaining stability or control during Feet at Wall Side Kick.
  - *Correction*: Focus on stabilizing through the core muscles, ensuring proper alignment of the shoulders, hips, and legs against the wall. Keep the movement controlled and avoid overarching or rounding of the lower back to maintain stability throughout the exercise.

Feet at Wall Inner Thigh Lift

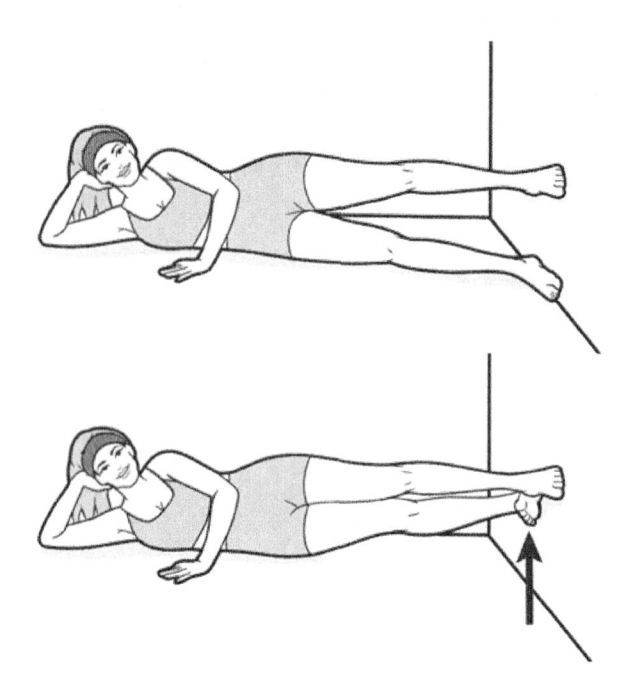

Closely related to the Side Kick, this exercise comprehensively works the core by engaging the abdominals, obliques, hip flexors, quadriceps, adductors, and glutes. The key variation here involves activating the adductors (inner thigh muscles) rather than the abductors, as you lift the lower leg toward the upper leg. Emphasizing slow, controlled movements is crucial for effectiveness.

Steps
1. Start by lying on your side with your head turned away from the wall.
2. Place the foot of your upper leg flat against the wall, slightly ahead of your torso.
3. Use your elbow or hand beneath the side of your neck for head support, and place your other arm on the floor in front of you for extra stability.
4. With your upper leg firmly pressed against the wall, inhale deeply.
5. As you exhale, lift your lower leg toward the upper leg, keeping your knee straight.
6. Inhale again as you gently lower your leg back to the starting position.
7. Continue to breathe in and out with each lift, actively engaging your core muscles.
8. Keep your hips aligned, ensuring one is directly over the other throughout the exercise.
9. Complete 15-20 lifts with the lower leg, then switch sides to ensure both legs are worked evenly.

Modifications
- For an easier version, raise the leg to a lower height or bend the knee slightly.
- To make the exercise more challenging, perform an additional set.

Problem Solving and Correction

- Problem: Difficulty maintaining stability or control during Feet at Wall Inner Thigh Lift.
  - *Correction*: Focus on stabilizing through the core muscles, ensuring proper alignment of the shoulders, hips, and legs against the wall. Keep the movement controlled and avoid overarching or rounding of the lower back to maintain stability throughout the exercise.
- Problem: Excessive arching or rounding of the lower back, causing strain or discomfort in the lower back.
  - *Correction*: Prioritize maintaining a neutral spine position by engaging the core muscles and avoiding excessive arching or rounding of the lower back. Press the lower back gently into the ground to support the spine and alleviate strain during the exercise.

Feet at Wall Hip Lift

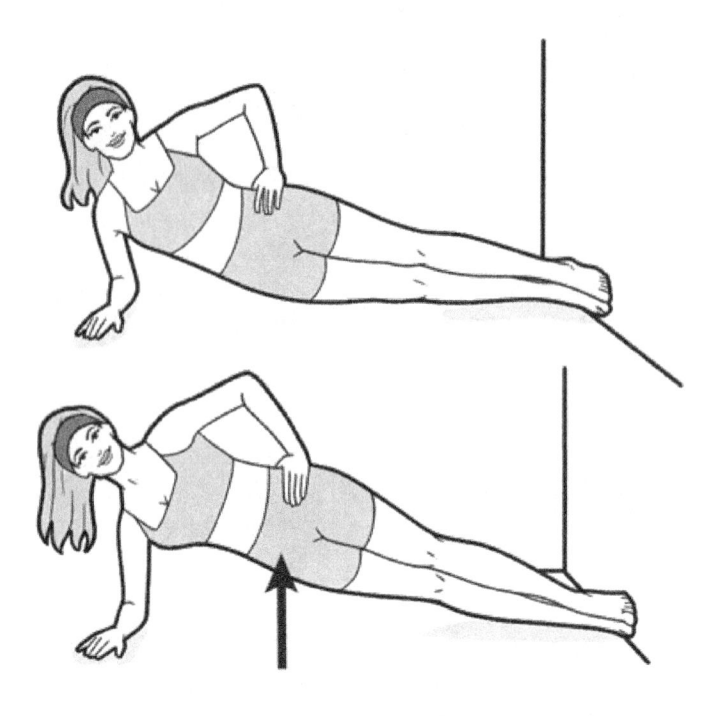

This workout targets the abdominals and obliques while engaging stabilization muscles around the torso. Its full-body approach and the required flexion in the midsection demand tight abs and glutes throughout the exercise, making it a comprehensive and challenging routine.

Steps
1. Start by lying on your side with your head away from the wall, ensuring both feet are flat against the wall and in line with your body.
2. Prop your upper body up on your elbow and place your other hand on your hip or the floor in front of you for balance.
3. Make sure your hips are stacked vertically.
4. Take a deep breath in, then, as you breathe out, tighten your abdominal and glute muscles to lift your hips off the ground.
5. Maintain this lifted position for two full breath cycles (inhaling and exhaling twice) before gently lowering your hips back to the floor.
6. Concentrate on maintaining a straight body line and engaging your core throughout the movement with steady breathing.
7. Complete 5-8 hip lifts on this side, then switch to your other side to repeat the lifts.

Modifications
- For a less intense workout, bend your knees and lift your hips only slightly off the ground.
- To make the exercise more challenging, extend the duration of the hold and add more

repetitions.

Problem Solving and Correction
- Problem: Difficulty maintaining stability or control during Feet at Wall Hip Lift, leaving you at higher risk of injury.
  - ***Correction***: Focus on stabilizing through the core muscles, ensuring proper alignment of the shoulders, hips, and legs against the wall. Keep the movement controlled and avoid overarching or rounding of the lower back to maintain stability throughout the exercise.

Plank Mountain Climbers

This comprehensive full-body exercise emphasizes core strength, requiring balance, stability, and control. It primarily targets the abdominals, hip flexors, and obliques but also extensively involves the leg muscles and calves due to its full-body engagement. It's important to perform this exercise without rushing, maintaining continuous engagement of the abdominals and glutes.

Steps
1. Begin by standing and facing the wall, placing your hands flat against it.
2. Spread your fingers wide for improved support, and keep your arms straight, avoiding locking your elbows.
3. Walk your feet back until your hands bear a moderate amount of your body weight, ensuring your elbows remain straight.
4. Rise onto the balls of your feet.
5. Take a deep breath in, and then as you exhale, draw your navel toward your spine to activate your core muscles.
6. As you inhale again, exhale and lift one knee toward your chest, maintaining a straight spine, then gently lower that leg back to the starting position and switch to the other leg.
7. Concentrate on keeping your shoulder blades pulled back and down, avoiding any upward shrug toward your neck.
8. Complete this movement by alternating legs for 10-15 repetitions each.

Modifications
- To increase the difficulty, perform additional repetitions, include an extra set, or stand further back from the wall.

Problem Solving and Correction

- Problem: Difficulty maintaining stability or control during Plank Mountain Climbers.
  - *Correction*: Focus on stabilizing through the core muscles, ensuring proper alignment of the shoulders, hips, and legs in the plank position. Maintain a strong plank position throughout the movement, avoiding sagging or lifting the hips to enhance stability and control.
- Problem: Experiencing fatigue or discomfort in the shoulders or arms due to misalignment of positioning.
  - *Correction*: Ensure proper alignment of the shoulders directly over the wrists and distribute weight evenly through the arms. Avoid shrugging the shoulders and maintain engagement of the shoulder blades to support the upper body. Take breaks as needed to prevent excessive fatigue in the shoulders and arms.

Standing Bird Dog

The Standing Bird Dog exercise tests your body asymmetrically, requiring the stabilization muscles across the torso to be fully engaged. It primarily targets the abdominals and obliques, but this standing wall Pilates variant also significantly involves the leg muscles, with the arms engaged to a lesser extent.

Steps
1. Face the wall, place your hands against it, and spread your fingers wide for stability. Keep your arms straight without locking your elbows.
2. Walk your feet back until your hands support a moderate amount of your body weight, ensuring your elbows remain straight.
3. Take a deep breath in.
4. As you breathe out, draw your navel toward your spine to activate your core.
5. Lift one arm up while simultaneously extending the opposite leg back in a smooth, controlled manner.
6. Return to the initial wall plank stance and then switch, lifting the alternate arm and leg.
7. Concentrate on drawing your navel in, maintaining your hips and shoulders in a straight line parallel to the wall, and breathing evenly.
8. Complete 8-10 sets of alternating lifts on each side.

Modifications
- Performing smaller arm lifts and leg reaches can make the exercise less intense.
- Add more repetitions, include an extra set, or lower your torso slightly to increase the challenge.

Problem Solving and Correction

- Problem: Experiencing difficulty coordinating arm and leg movements.
  - *Correction*: Start with slow, controlled movements and focus on engaging the correct muscles. Concentrate on extending the opposite arm and leg while maintaining balance and stability through the core. Gradually increase the speed of the movement as coordination improves.

Feet at Wall Plank

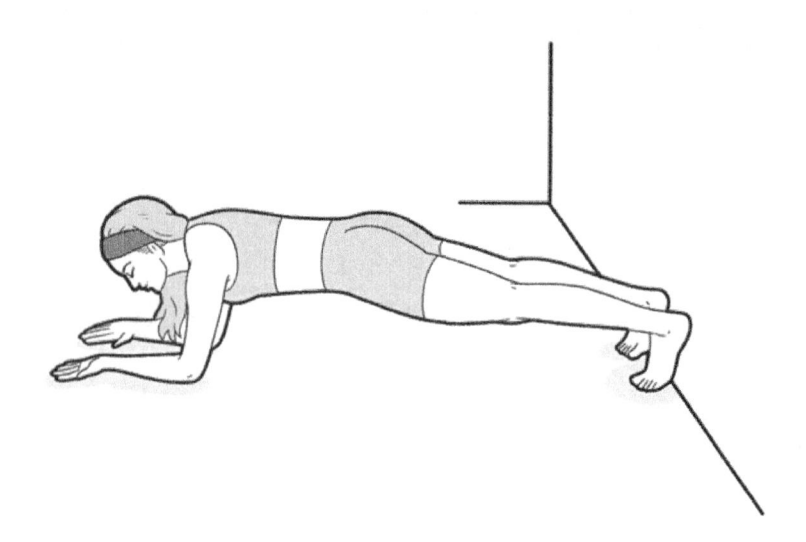

This fundamental core exercise targets the abdominals, obliques, and various stabilizing muscles. Utilizing the wall enhances stability, particularly in forward and backward movements, enabling a more solid and efficient plank hold.

Steps
1. Start by positioning yourself on the floor with your feet against the wall, initially on your knees, as you set your forearms in place.
2. Take a deep breath in. As you breathe out, tighten your abdominal muscles and clench your glutes.
3. Lift your body into a forearm plank, pushing your feet firmly against the wall.
4. Ensure your tailbone is tucked under, aiming for a straight back, though a slight curve where your abdominals are drawn in is acceptable.
5. Continue breathing in and out, maintaining tightness in your core muscles.
6. Keep your shoulders pulled down away from your ears and focus on maintaining proper spinal alignment.
7. Aim to hold this plank position for 30-60 seconds.

Modifications
- For a lighter workout, reduce the duration of your hold or drop to your knees.
- To amp up the difficulty, raise your feet higher on the wall or switch to a straight-arm plank.

Problem Solving and Correction
- Problem: Experiencing strain or discomfort in the shoulders or arms due to lack of

engagement of the appropriate stabilization muscles.
- *Correction*: Ensure proper alignment of the shoulders and distribute weight evenly through the arms pressing into the ground. Avoid shrugging the shoulders and maintain a slight bend in the elbows to reduce strain on the arms. Focus on engaging the upper back muscles to support the shoulders and maintain stability.
- Problem: Unable to maintain balance with feet against the wall.
  - *Correction*: Start with a lower incline against the wall to reduce the challenge and gradually progress to a higher incline as strength and stability improve. Focus on engaging the core muscles and maintaining a strong plank position to support balance and stability.

Feet at Wall Side Plank

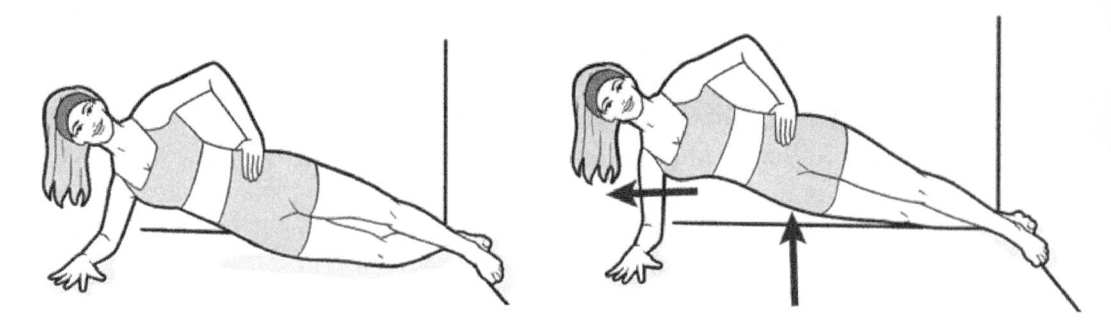

This variation focuses on strengthening the oblique abdominal muscles and enhancing your balance. Beginners should first develop the necessary strength and balance through oblique warm-ups and modified side planks before advancing to the full side plank position.

Steps
8. Start by lying on one side on the floor, with your hips on the ground, supporting yourself on one forearm, knees slightly bent, and keeping your spine straight.
9. Breathe in and out, then lift yourself into a side plank by pressing your feet against the wall, straightening your knees, and lifting your hips off the ground.
10. Ensure your glutes are engaged and your body forms a straight line from head to toe, with your hips aligned under your shoulders.
11. Concentrate on elevating your body by engaging your core and actively pushing the ground away with your supporting arm.
12. Maintain this position for 30-60 seconds, focusing on steady breathing and keeping your core muscles tight.

Modifications
- For an easier variation, bend your knees and do the side plank while resting on them.
- To make it harder, do the side plank resting on your hand with your arm fully extended.
- For the highest difficulty level, lift your top leg away from your bottom leg and extend your top arm straight up, forming a star shape with your body.

Problem Solving and Correction
- Problem: Difficulty maintaining alignment of the hips, putting your lower back at risk of injury or strain.
  - **Correction**: Concentrate on vertically stacking the hips and shoulders to maintain proper alignment. Engage the core muscles to prevent the hips from sinking or rotating. Focus on lifting the hips toward the ceiling to maintain a straight line from head to heels.
- Problem: Unable to hold the position for an extended period due to lack of required

stability.
- ***Correction***: Start with shorter hold times and gradually increase the duration as strength and stability improve. Focus on breathing evenly and engaging the core muscles throughout the hold. Alternatively, perform the exercise with the feet placed on the ground to reduce the intensity until sufficient strength is developed.

Feet at Wall Side Stretch

This dynamic stretch emphasizes core engagement and resembles a classic yoga movement. It provides a deep stretch along the side of your body while also strengthening the core as you hold a side plank position. It's crucial to keep your core and glutes tightly engaged throughout the entire movement for stability and effectiveness.

Steps
1. Start by positioning yourself on your side, propped up on a straight arm, with your feet against the wall and knees slightly bent.
2. Take a deep breath in and out.
3. As you exhale, press your feet into the wall, activate your core and glutes, straighten your legs, and lift your hips off the ground into a side plank.
4. At the same time, reach your free arm overhead in a sweeping motion.
5. Hold this position for a second as you feel the stretch all down the top side of your body.
6. Inhale and gently lower your hips back to the floor. Exhale and lift into the side plank again.
7. Perform this lifting motion 5-8 times on one side, then switch to repeat the sequence on the opposite side.
8. Concentrate on keeping your core tight, moving smoothly, maintaining balance on your side, and ensuring proper alignment throughout the exercise.

Modifications
- For a simpler version, perform the exercise on your forearm rather than supporting yourself on your hand with a straight arm.
- Due to its level of challenge, it may be best to attempt this exercise after completing 5-10 wall Pilates sessions.

Problem Solving and Correction
- Problem: Difficulty maintaining stability or control during Feet At Wall Side Stretch.

- *Correction*: Focus on stabilizing through the core muscles, ensuring proper alignment of the shoulders, hips, and legs against the wall. Keep the movement controlled and avoid overarching or rounding of the lower back to maintain stability throughout the exercise.
- Problem: Limited flexibility or range of motion in the lateral stretch, meaning you are unable to get into the full position.
  - *Correction*: Start with a smaller range of motion for the lateral stretch and gradually increase it as flexibility improves. Focus on lengthening through the side body while maintaining stability through the core. Incorporate regular stretching exercises to improve flexibility over time.

Roll-Down to Walkout Plank

This comprehensive exercise stretches and lengthens the entire backside of your body. Starting with a roll-down, it lengthens the spine, progressing to a walkout that stretches the glutes and hamstrings. The final plank position activates the core, demanding stability throughout the torso.

Steps
1. Begin by standing up straight with your back against the wall, positioning your feet 6 inches from the wall, and bending your knees slightly.
2. Take a deep breath in, and as you exhale, start to lower your head, bringing your chin toward your chest.
3. Continue curling your body forward and slowly rolling down toward the floor, vertebra by vertebra, allowing your buttocks to remain against the wall for added stability.
4. Place your hands on the floor and gradually walk them forward until you reach a plank position. Keep your legs as straight as possible during this walkout, though a slight knee bend is acceptable if needed.
5. Once in the plank, hold the position for a cycle of one breath in and out, then walk your hands back toward your feet and slowly roll upward back to a standing position.
6. Complete 3-5 repetitions of this roll-down to plank walkout exercise.
7. Concentrate on maintaining steady breathing, engaging your core, and minimizing any side-to-side or twisting movements throughout the exercise.

Modifications
- For a simpler variation, lower yourself onto your knees once you've reached the plank position, and maintain the plank from this knee-supported stance.

Problem Solving and Correction

- Problem: Difficulty maintaining stability or control during Roll-Down To Walkout Plank.
  - *Correction*: Focus on engaging the core muscles throughout the movement, ensuring proper alignment of the spine and hips. Keep the movement controlled and avoid overarching or rounding of the back to maintain stability from the standing position to the plank position.
- Problem: Limited flexibility or mobility in the roll-down, meaning you are unable to reach the floor with straight legs.
  - *Correction*: Before attempting the exercise, perform gentle stretches for the hamstrings and spine to improve flexibility and mobility. Focus on initiating the roll-down movement from the upper back and gradually work toward touching the floor with the hands while keeping the legs straight.

Mermaid Stretch

The Mermaid Stretch is designed to elongate and open up the sides of the body. By anchoring firmly on the ground while stretching the arm up and over, the stretch effectively connects through the body's center. This exercise also teaches the importance of keeping the shoulder blades stable and in place as the arm extends.

Steps
1. Start by sitting upright, ensuring your back is straight, positioned next to the wall, with your shoulder around one arm's length away.
2. Arrange your legs in an 'S' shape, with one knee bent in front of you and the other bent behind (refer to the illustration for guidance).
3. With the arm nearest the wall, reach out and touch the wall as the starting position.
4. Take a deep breath in. As you exhale, lift the arm that is touching the wall upward and then over your head, stretching your body to the side away from the wall.
5. Hold this side bend briefly before gently returning to your initial sitting position.
6. Inhale while raising your arm and exhale deeply as you extend into the stretch, feeling it along the side of your torso.
7. Complete this stretch 3 times before switching sides to ensure a balanced workout.

Modifications
- If the stretch feels too intense, shorten the distance you reach with your arm.

Problem Solving and Correction
- Problem: Difficulty achieving proper alignment or range of motion during the Mermaid Stretch.

- ***Correction***: Focus on sitting tall and lengthening through the spine before initiating the lateral stretch. Engage the core muscles to stabilize the torso and support the proper alignment of the shoulders, hips, and spine. Gradually increase the stretch while maintaining proper form, and avoid forcing the movement beyond your current range of motion.

Rotational Stretch

This stretch enhances thoracic (mid-back) mobility, which is crucial for maintaining good posture, an upright stance, and efficient breathing. Incorporating a wall into this exercise helps you achieve and hold a deeper stretch more effectively.

Steps
1. Start by sitting on the floor on your mat, positioning your back about a foot away from the wall in a cross-legged posture.
2. Take a deep breath in. As you exhale, twist your torso toward one side, extending the leading arm first toward your knee and then reaching back to place your hand on the wall, further rotating your body toward it.
3. Breathe in and out again before gently returning to your initial, forward-facing position.
4. Proceed to perform the rotation toward the opposite side.
5. Maintain an upright spine and ensure deep breathing throughout the stretch.
6. It's okay to turn your head as part of the rotation if it feels comfortable.
7. Complete 3 stretches in each direction.

Modifications
- For a milder stretch, reduce the extent of your torso rotation.

Problem Solving and Correction
- Problem: Difficulty maintaining proper form or alignment during the Rotational Stretch.
  - **Correction**: Focus on stabilizing through the core muscles and maintaining a tall spine throughout the movement. Engage the abdominals and back muscles to support proper alignment of the shoulders, hips, and spine. Start with smaller rotational movements and gradually increase the range of motion as flexibility and control improve.

- Problem: Feeling strain or discomfort in the shoulders, back, or hips.
  - ***Correction***: Ensure that the rotational movement is executed smoothly and within a comfortable range of motion. Avoid forcing the stretch beyond your current flexibility level, and listen to your body to avoid overstretching or straining the muscles. Use props such as yoga blocks or bolsters for support if needed.

28-DAY AB TRANSFORMATION CHALLENGE

Now that you have read through the wall Pilates exercises and hopefully tried them successfully, it's time to get serious. If you're ready for the 28-day Ab Transformation Challenge, I've developed 6 workouts of varying difficulty and intensity: low-intensity, moderate-intensity, high-intensity interval training (HIIT), the long one, arm day, and leg day. Several rest days are built into this program but feel free to modify them as needed.

The goal of the challenge is to get fitter, stronger, and better at Pilates. However, the real goal of the challenge is to complete it. Over the 28-day workout calendar, there are only seven rest days, meaning there will be 21 workout days in a month. This isn't easy. Don't be hard on yourself if you can't complete every workout or don't have the time. Missing a day here or there isn't an issue because you will still see results as long as you can consistently string together a good run of days.

The challenge is called the Ab Transformation challenge due to the heavy focus on core and the high number of calories burned during the 28 days. Remember, you won't see results after one day, but if you train consistently, eat fewer calories than you are burning, and maintain proper form throughout your workouts, you will soon see great results.

These six wall Pilates workouts are suggestions; you should mix them up as you wish. I've compiled them based on my experience as a Pilates mat instructor, so they will help you reach your goals effectively, but that doesn't mean you can't amend them to better fit into your lifestyle.

I recommend doing all six exercises from the warm-up every workout. However, as you become more familiar with breathing and spinal alignment, it can be shortened (performed in 3-5 minutes total) and used mainly for centering purposes.

The HIIT workout is a pick-your-poison type where you can choose which exercises from each group (though specific numbers are advised) and get a new workout every time. You may even want to combine workouts or add another HIIT day as your fitness level improves.

Following the list of workouts, you will see a quick reference table with all the exercises that you can use to perform the workouts. Let's get busy and get fit!

Workout #1: Low-Intensity

- Warm-up: All 6 exercises.
- Upper body: #7, 8.
- Lower body: #17, 21.
- Core: #30, 31, 32, 33, 38, 39, 40, 41, 43, 44, 49, 50.
- Time: 25-35 minutes.

Workout #2: Moderate-Intensity

- Warm-up: All 6 exercises.
- Upper body: #7, 8, 9, 10, 11.
- Lower body: #14, 15, 17, 20, 21, 22, 24, 25, 26, 27.
- Core: #30, 31, 32, 33, 35, 37, 38, 39, 40, 41, 42, 43, 44, 45, 46, 48, 49, 50.
- Time: 45-55 minutes.

Workout #3: High-Intensity Interval Training (HIIT)

- Warm-up: All 6 exercises.
- Upper body: Pick 3 exercises.
- Lower body: Pick 4-5 exercises.
- Core: Pick 5-6 exercises (but not #49 or 50).
- Time: After the warm-up, each exercise will be timed. Interval training consists of ON time for performing the chosen exercise, and OFF time is your rest between exercises. You will do 40 seconds ON (exercise) and 20 seconds OFF (resting). Total time 20-28 minutes, depending on the number of intervals you do.

Workout #4: Mix and Match

- Warm-up: All 6 exercises.
- Upper body: Pick half of the exercises. Modify as needed.
- Lower body: Pick half of the exercises. Modify as needed.
- Core: Pick half of the exercises. Modify as needed.
- Time: 55-65 minutes.

Workout #5: Arm Day

- Warm-up: All 6 exercises.
- Upper body: All 7 exercises. Modify as needed.

- Core: #33, 34, 35, 36, 37, 43, 44, 45, 46, 47, 48, 49, 50.
- Time: 30-40 minutes.

Workout #6: Leg Day

- Warm-up: All 6 exercises.
- Lower body: All 16 exercises. Modify as needed.
- Core: #30, 31, 39, 40, 41, 42, 43, 44, 45, 46, 47, 49, 50.
- Time: 40-50 minutes.

28-Day Workout Calendar

DAY	1	2	3	4	5	6	7
WORKOUT	#1	#5	Rest/Walk	#1	#6	Rest/Walk	#2
DAY	8	9	10	11	12	13	14
WORKOUT	#3	Rest/Walk	#4	#1	#5	Rest/Walk	#2
DAY	15	16	17	18	19	20	21
WORKOUT	#6	#3	Rest/Walk	#4	#1	#5	Rest/Walk
DAY	22	23	24	25	26	27	28
WORKOUT	#2	#6	#1	Rest/Walk	#3	#5	#4

EXERCISE QUICK REFERENCE TABLE

1. Breathing and Spinal Alignment	2. Side Bend Stretch	3. Forward Bend Stretch	4. Chest Opener	5. Double Arm Reach	6. Roll-Down
7. Standing Plank	8. Plank With Arm Reaches	9. Plank Walks	10. Plank Shoulder Taps	11. Push-Up	12. Single Arm Push-Up
13. Tricep Side Push-Up	14. Standing Leg Kicks	15. Standing Side Leg Kick	16. Standing Side Leg Circles	17. Wall Squat	18. Partial Squat With Leg Extension
19. Partial Squat With Knee Lift	20. Wall Squat With Heel Lift	21. Bridge	22. Bridge With Knee Lift	23. Bridge With Straight Leg Lift	24. Wall Scissors
25. Bridge With Knee to Chest	26. Bridge With Knee Circles	27. Kneeling With Side Leg Kick	28. Kneeling With Pendulum Kick	29. Kneeling With Side Leg Circles	30. Single Knee Stretch

31. Single Straight Leg Stretch	32. Cross Over	33. Hands on Wall Toe Taps	34. Hands on Wall Both Legs Lower	35. Hands on Wall Single Leg Stretch	36. Hands on Wall Double Leg Stretch
37. Hands on Wall Scissors	38. Feet at Wall "The Hundred"	39. Feet at Wall Pendulum Kick	40. Feet at Wall Side Kick	41. Feet at Wall Inner Thigh Lift	42. Feet at Wall Hip Lift
43. Plank Mountain Climbers	44. Standing Bird Dog	45. Feet at Wall Plank	46. Feet at Wall Side Plank	47. Feet at Wall Side Stretch	48. Roll-Down to Walkout Plank

49. Mermaid Stretch	50. Rotational Stretch

CONCLUSION: PLAN FOR CONSISTENCY

Congratulations on completing this book! Embarking on your journey with wall Pilates marks a transformative step toward integrating a powerful practice into your daily life. The benefits of Pilates are immense, yet they only unfold through dedicated and consistent effort. With the knowledge gained from this book, you're now better prepared to lead a more joyful and healthier life.

It's important to remember that a balanced approach to physical activity is key to a wholesome lifestyle. A blend of activities like walking, swimming, resistance training, yoga, and Pilates not only enhances health and fitness but also enriches your life with variety. For those seeking improvements in strength, flexibility, functional mobility, balance, and body composition, persistence in your wall Pilates practice is crucial.

As a practitioner of Pilates, I urge you to delve deeper into its benefits and continue exploring how it can positively impact your life. The journey to mastering the mind-body connection is a lifelong endeavor, with endless learning opportunities along the way.

Pilates, adaptable in intensity, can be practiced daily, allowing you to listen to your body and adjust your routine accordingly. It's advisable to start slowly, allowing for recovery time, and to focus initially on mastering proper form. Incorporating Pilates into your routine and treating it as a daily appointment on your calendar will help cultivate consistency.

As you move forward, be kind to yourself. Perfection is not the goal; progress is. Everyone's journey with diet and exercise is unique, but with consistent effort and the use of all the tools at your disposal, you will see results. Celebrate each step you take in this journey, recognizing the positive changes and the strength you're building, both inside and out. Here's to a healthier, happier you with wall Pilates—may your practice bring you strength, serenity, and joy.

If this book has guided you closer to your wellness goals, inspired a new perspective on exercise, or helped you find a deeper connection with your body through wall Pilates, I would be grateful if you took a moment to leave a review. Your feedback not only supports my work but also helps others discover the transformative power of Pilates. Share your journey, the challenges you've overcome, and the victories you've celebrated. Let's spread the word and inspire more people to embark on their own path to wellness.

VIDEO DEMONSTRATIONS PASSWORD

ex89em67

How to Access the Videos:

1. Scan the QR code below with your phone.
2. Enter the password.

If you have any issues accessing the videos, please email me at evimatonis@gmail.com.

REFERENCES

CDC. (2019). Finding a Balance. Centers for Disease Control and Prevention. https://www.cdc.gov/healthyweight/calories/index.html

CDC. (2019, December 4). Target Heart Rate and Estimated Maximum Heart Rate | Physical Activity | CDC. https://www.cdc.gov/physicalactivity/basics/measuring/heartrate.htm

Bogh, A. F., Jensen, S. B. K., Juhl, C. R., Janus, C., Sandsdal, R. M., Lundgren, J. R., Noer, M. H., Vu, N. Q., Fiorenza, M., Stallknecht, B. M., Holst, J. J., Madsbad, S., & Torekov, S. S. (2022). Insufficient sleep predicts poor weight loss maintenance after 1 year. Sleep. https://doi.org/10.1093/sleep/zsac295

Dicken, S. J., & Batterham, R. L. (2024). Ultra-processed Food and Obesity: What Is the Evidence? Current Nutrition Reports. https://doi.org/10.1007/s13668-024-00517-z

Di Lorenzo, C. E. (2011). Pilates: What Is It? Should It Be Used in Rehabilitation? Sports Health: A Multidisciplinary Approach, 3(4), 352–361. https://doi.org/10.1177/1941738111410285

Fogelman, N., Magin, Z., Hart, R., & Sinha, R. (2020). A Longitudinal Study of Life Trauma, Chronic Stress and Body Mass Index on Weight Gain over a 2-Year Period. Behavioral Medicine, 1–9. https://doi.org/10.1080/08964289.2020.1780192

Greger, M. (2020). A Whole Food Plant-Based Diet Is Effective for Weight Loss: The Evidence. American Journal of Lifestyle Medicine, 14(5), 155982762091240. https://doi.org/10.1177/1559827620912400

Kim, J. Y. (2020). Optimal diet strategies for weight loss and weight loss maintenance. Journal of Obesity & Metabolic Syndrome, 30(1). https://doi.org/10.7570/jomes20065

Lim, E. J., & Park, J. E. (2019). The effects of Pilates and yoga participants on engagement in functional movement and individual health level. Journal of Exercise Rehabilitation, 15(4), 553–559. https://doi.org/10.12965/jer.1938280.140

Tolnai, N., Szabó, Z., Köteles, F., & Szabo, A. (2016). Physical and psychological benefits of once-a-week Pilates exercises in young sedentary women: A 10-week longitudinal study. Physiology & Behavior, 163, 211–218. https://doi.org/10.1016/j.physbeh.2016.05.025

Printed in Great Britain
by Amazon